Religion in Contemporary Society
for AS students

by Wendy Dossett,
Karl Lawson, Roger J Owen,
Andrew Pearce

Series Editor: Roger J Owen

Religion in Contemporary Society

Religion in Contemporary Society

Roger J. Owen, Series Editor

Roger J. Owen was Head of RE in a variety of schools for thirty years, as well as being a Head of Faculty, advisory teacher for primary and secondary RE, Section 23 Inspector and 'O' Level and GCSE Chief Examiner. Author of seventeen educational titles, he was WJEC Religious Studies AS and A2 Chair of Examiners until 2008.

Acknowledgements

The author and publishers would like to thank the following for permission to reproduce copyright material in this book:

akg-images, p96r, p100; akg-images/Rabatti Domingie, p108t; ©Greg Balfour Evans /Alamy, p2; © Malcolm Case-Green/Alamy, p8; © Squint/Alamy, p36 l; ©Coaster/Alamy, p36r; © James Boardman / Alamy, p37; ©Geoff A. Howard /Alamy, p40; The Photolibrary Wales /Alamy, p58t; ©Pictorial Press Ltd /Alamy, p59; © Posh Parker / Alamy, p61 tl; MarioPonti /Alamy, p61 tr; wales_heritage_photos /Alamy, p69; Jeff Morgan Hay on Wye/Alamy, p73 l; Libby Welch /Alamy, p86; © Mary Evans Picture Library / Alamy, p88, p97; ©The Print Collector / Alamy, p96 l; © INTERFOTO Pressebildagentur /Alamy, p106 ; The Art Archive / Gianni Dagli Orti, p15; BBC Photolibrary, p58b, p64t, p64bl, p75; BBC Worldwide, p63, p64t; Capital Pictures: p44, p47t, p47b, p48t, p48b, p50, p52, p53t, p53b; Church in Wales, p77; ©Sion Touhig / Sygma / Corbis, p91; © Daniel W Erlander, p98; General Medical Council, p4; iStockphoto, p18, p23, p35, p42, p55b, p80, p109t; The Library of Congress, p55t; P A Archive / PA Photos, p3t, p3b; The Canadian Press / PA Photos p24; AP / PA Photos, p82; Photolibrary Wales, p72; Punch Ltd, punch.co.uk, p78; Raghu Rai / Magnum Photos, p87; By kind permission of Alister McGrath, Photo: Nigel Bovey, p73r; Ofcom, p56; © Science Museum / Science & Society, p20; New Line/Saul Zaenetz/ Wingnut /The Kobal Collection/ Vinet, Pierre, P109b.

Every effort has been made to contact copyright holders of material reproduced in this publication. Any omission will be rectified in subsequent printing if notice is given to the publisher. While the information in this publication is believed to be true and accurate at the date of going to press, neither the author nor the publisher can accept any legal responsibility for any errors or omissions that may have been made.

Published by UWIC Press
UWIC, Cyncoed Road,
Cardiff CF23 6XD
cgrove@uwic.ac.uk
029 2041 6515

ISBN   978-1-905617-79-1

Sponsored by the Welsh Assembly Government

Design by *the info group*
Picture research by *Picture Research Wales*
Printed by *HSW Print*

Front cover image: www.istockphoto.com

Religion in Contemporary Society for AS students

by Wendy Dossett,
Karl Lawson, Roger J Owen,
Andrew Pearce

Series Editor: Roger J Owen

Contents

Religion in Contemporary Society

Introduction

This book assumes no prior knowledge about Religion in Contemporary Society and presents the various constituent elements in such a way as to meet the requirements of the WJEC AS Specification. However, under no circumstances should this book be used as the sole textbook for the course, since advanced study requires the skills of wide reading and the analysis of a range of views on different issues.

The book is designed to be used in tandem with the teachers' book, which provides more detailed background information on some of the topics covered and assistance with the tasks that appear in the text.

AS level candidates are expected to demonstrate not only knowledge and understanding but also certain skills, such as the ability to analyse and evaluate different views. Some of the tasks that appear in this book are designed to assist in developing those skills. Teachers and students will doubtless think of others.

This book, as well as the accompanying teachers' book, is constructed with Key Skills in mind. Students are asked to develop communication skills by taking part in discussions, gathering information and writing. They are asked to develop ICT skills through encouragement to make critically-aware use of the Internet and to present findings in the form of class presentations. They are asked to solve problems through making cases for particular viewpoints and to work with others on joint research tasks.

The students' and teachers' books both attempt to reflect the variety of views on euthanasia and animal rights, the presentation of religion on television, the state and influence of religion in society and psychological understanding of religious belief. Not only is appreciation of the diversity of views a requirement of the WJEC AS Specification, but it is also crucial to a proper, rounded understanding of religion in contemporary society. All religious traditions contain a range of viewpoints, beliefs and practices and students should be able to demonstrate a critical, yet non-judgmental, awareness of this fact.

Four quite distinctive areas are included in this book: morality, media, sociology and psychology. The content of the book aims, as the WJEC course does, to give a broad introduction to religious perspectives on these four key aspects of contemporary society that are significant in human experience. The topics covered are exemplars of these key aspects.

Medical and Environmental Ethics

Aim of the section

This section asks you to consider the diversity of ideas about one medical and one environmental issue, namely:

▶ **Euthanasia**

▶ **Animal Rights.**

This means you will have to consider the following key matters:

▶ the definition of euthanasia;

▶ the legality and varying types of euthanasia;

▶ arguments both for and against euthanasia (including the hospice movement, and the concepts of sanctity and quality of life);

▶ the varying views on the moral status of animals;

▶ arguments both for and against using animals for food, medical and non-medical experimentation, hunting, culling, or as pets and entertainment, (including the concepts of speciesism and stewardship).

You are asked to study these issues from the perspective of at least one major world religion.

Euthanasia

Aim

After studying this chapter you should be able to show a clear knowledge and understanding of: the term 'euthanasia'; the difference between active and passive euthanasia; the legal position of euthanasia in the UK; and the difference between voluntary and non-voluntary euthanasia. You should also be able to understand the contrasting arguments both for and against euthanasia and be able to determine to what extent euthanasia is compatible with religious principles.

What is euthanasia?

The term euthanasia comes from two Greek words: *eu*, meaning 'well', and *thanatos* meaning 'death' - and means 'painless, happy death'. Literally 'a good death', it describes a medical procedure by which a person terminates his or her own life because of extreme pain or suffering, or by which the life of another person is either allowed to come to an end or is brought to an end, with legal consent, because of a critical medical condition.

Two important distinctions are made about the way euthanasia is performed:

passive euthanasia: to allow a patient to die by withdrawing medical treatment or nourishment, for example turning off a life-support system to which a patient in a coma has been connected;

active euthanasia: to take action deliberately designed to end a patient's life, for example giving someone a lethal injection or, in time of war, a mortally wounded soldier in great pain asking his comrade to 'finish him off' in order to shorten his suffering.

Task

Research and presentation task	Using the Internet to explore the issues of active/passive euthanasia:
	(a) Go to the website:
	www.bbc.co.uk/religion/ethics/euthanasia/overview/activepassive_1
	and read the information contained here.
	(b) Produce a presentation outlining your views on whether 'passive euthanasia is more morally acceptable than active euthanasia'.

The current legal position on euthanasia in the UK

As the law stands in the UK, deliberate or 'active' euthanasia will normally leave anyone assisting suicide or death liable for murder. Euthanasia is outlawed by the Murder Act of 1965 and by the Suicide Act of 1971. The Murder Act states that intentional killing, even with the patient's consent for compassionate reasons, is a crime and the Suicide Act makes assisted suicide a crime. The House of Lords ruled in 1994 that 'there should be no change in the law to permit euthanasia.'

However, euthanasia has been decriminalised in a number of European countries, such as the Netherlands and Belgium, and in 2008 these countries were joined by Luxembourg. In Luxembourg, for example, euthanasia is allowed only for the terminally ill, who have expressed their desire to die, and where the consent of two doctors and a panel of experts has been given.

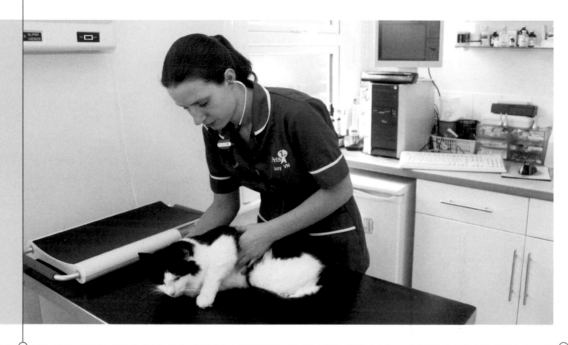

Why do we allow 'active' animal euthanasia but reject 'active' human euthanasia?

Seminar topic

Why do you think active euthanasia is illegal in the UK?

We are now going to consider two of the main forms of euthanasia:
1 **voluntary euthanasia;**   2 **non-voluntary euthanasia.**

1 Voluntary euthanasia

This means causing a patient's death, where consent has been given by the individual. Most groups currently campaigning for changes in the law to allow euthanasia are campaigning for voluntary euthanasia, i.e. euthanasia carried out at the specific request and consent of the dying person. Those campaigning for voluntary euthanasia in the UK include the 'Dignity in Dying' organisation (formerly the Voluntary Euthanasia Society) which states that its vision is:

> *'for everyone to be guaranteed choice and dignity at the end of their life . . . and include a legal right to effective pain relief to help ease suffering. We want end-of-life decision making to be open and honest, and firmly under the control of the patient.*
>
> *We want a full range of choices to be available to terminally ill people including medically assisted dying within strict legal safeguards. Such legal safeguards would also protect the vulnerable and remove the conditions that give rise to unchecked euthanasia and 'mercy killings.'*

Diane Pretty desperately wanted a doctor or her husband to help her to die. Motor neurone disease left her mind sharp but gradually destroyed her muscles, making it hard for her to communicate with her family. It left her in a wheelchair, catheterised and fed through a tube. Diane fought against the disease for the last two years of her life and had every possible medical treatment. Rather than living with the fear of dying by choking or suffocation, she wanted her husband to help her die, although this would be classed as assisted suicide and is illegal in the United Kingdom.

Pretty took her case to court, using the Human Rights Act to argue that the Director of Public Prosecutions should make a commitment not to prosecute anybody involved in helping her to die. British courts did not accept Pretty's arguments, with the House of Lords, Britain's highest court, eventually turning her case down. The European Court of Human Rights refused to acknowledge that the European Convention on Human Rights provided a right to die, and her appeal to that court also failed.

Did Diane Pretty die with dignity?

2 Non-voluntary euthanasia

This is the killing of a patient who is not able to express his/her wishes about whether they should be able to live or die (for example newborn babies; or a person severely brain-damaged and in a long-term coma with no awareness of their surroundings referred to as a Permanent Vegetative State). The issue of PVS is often linked to the idea of 'personhood'.

The question often linked with non-voluntary euthanasia is: 'At what point does someone cease to be a person and die?' This is a pertinent question, because if a patient has ceased to be 'a person' then this could seriously change our approach to non-voluntary euthanasia, as we are no longer killing a person.'

With the advancement of medical science the answer given to this question has changed considerably over the centuries. In the 17th Century, for example, a person was said to be dead when their heart and lungs stopped working. However, by the 20th Century the heart could be stopped during by-pass surgery, so this was no longer an adequate definition. Also, we now have respirators that can breathe for people – so that saying 'when they cease to breathe' is also no longer sufficient.

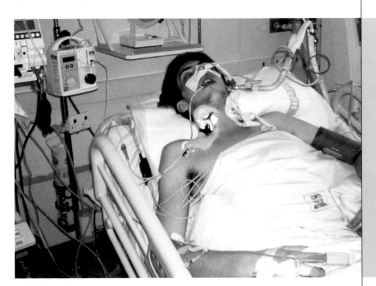

The most commonly accepted definition at present is when they are 'brain dead'. This, however, causes further debate: is it death of the whole brain, death of the higher brain

At what point does someone cease to be a person?

functions (consciousness, thought and feelings) or brainstem death (where a person needs a ventilator to breathe, and does not show specified reflexes which depend upon circuits within the brain)?

Seminar topic

Is euthanasia ever right in cases where the patient cannot give their consent?

Case study: Anthony Bland (1972-1993)

Anthony Bland was a 17-year-old victim of the 1989 Hillsborough Football Stadium disaster. He was left in a persistent vegetative state. PVS is a condition of patients with severe brain damage in whom coma has progressed to a state of wakefulness without detectable awareness. His parents believed that Anthony would not want to be kept alive in such a condition. The hospital, with the support of his parents, applied for a court order allowing him to 'die with dignity'. As a result he became the first patient in English legal history to be allowed to die by the courts through the withdrawal of life-prolonging treatment – hydration and artificial nutrition – which he did in 1993.

Task

Writing task

Look at the following examples and state whether they would involve voluntary or non-voluntary euthanasia and also whether they involve active or passive euthanasia:

a) A man who is in pain caused by a terminal disease asks his doctor for a lethal injection to end his pain.

b) A child is born with a severe disability and is incapable of feeding herself. The parents ask for her not to be fed.

c) A woman who is in hospital dying from a terminal disease asks not to be given food or water.

d) A man is in a permanent vegetative state and his family and doctors decide it would be best if he were given a lethal injection.

Arguments for legalising voluntary euthanasia

There has been a growing campaign by groups such as 'Dignity in Dying' to legalise voluntary euthanasia. A number of arguments (some of which might also apply to non-voluntary euthanasia) have been given in favour of euthanasia, including:

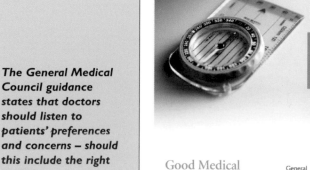

Good Medical Practice — General Medical Council

The General Medical Council guidance states that doctors should listen to patients' preferences and concerns – should this include the right to die?

1 Personal autonomy

The 'Good Medical Practice' guide for doctors (2006) issued by the General Medical Council states that doctors should listen to patients and respond to their concerns and preferences. They should also respect patients' rights to reach decisions with their doctor about their treatment and care. It should be a patient's own choice whether they live or die: some argue it is even a basic human right.

What right does society have to force people to stay alive? Are they being kept alive in order to fulfil their family's wishes and not their own? This argument is often linked with:

2 The 'quality of life' principle

Quality of life is a human condition in which a person enjoys a degree of physical, intellectual and emotional well-being, the absence of which through severe illness is sometimes used as an argument in favour of euthanasia. A person's standard of life could be continually diminishing and this would prevent them from having a decent existence. For example, they might lose their dignity by becoming incontinent or ending up reliant upon other people to care for them. Humans should be able to live their lives in a dignified manner until the end of their days. A person should also be able to ask 'What do I class as a dignified existence?' and be allowed to end their life if they think this is not met.

3 Euthanasia will end the person's suffering

Death, for many people, is often preceded by serious pain (emotional, physical and psychological), which can be prevented only to a limited extent by drugs. Is it not more humane, therefore, to quickly end a person's suffering? Other arguments which support legalising voluntary euthanasia include the principle of compassion – that in some circumstances it is the most loving thing to do.

4 Not allowing euthanasia will put extra pressure on society

With the breakdown of the traditional family unit in many societies, people are left with no one to care for them. Some argue that euthanasia is preferable to being left to die alone or putting pressure on the Health Service. There are not enough hospice placements for everyone and there is a need for organ transplants, when those dying could know that they are helping others to live. Also people often state that they would prefer death to dementia or Alzheimer's disease.

5 It shortens the suffering caused to the patient's family

People find that the drawn-out process of a serious or terminal illness can have a massive impact upon the emotional, physical and psychological well-being of the patient's spouse/partner, family and friends. Allowing a patient to die quickly would reduce the length of the suffering they have to endure.

6 Allowing euthanasia would allow us to legalise and regulate what already happens

Doctors can give their patients morphine to minimise pain, but they know that a side-effect of this is that it will hasten the patient's death. This is known as the Principle of Double Effect. When a person performs an action in order to achieve a good primary effect (consequence) they are not held responsible for any unintentional secondary effects. In this case the primary effect is to reduce the pain the patient is suffering, whereas the secondary and unintended consequence of this is that you also shorten the patient's life.

7 What is the difference between withdrawing treatment (passive euthanasia - which is legal) and delivering a lethal injection (active euthanasia – which is not)?

This argument states that if you allow one form you should allow the other. In fact, passive euthanasia could cause more suffering than active euthanasia, as the patient may live for longer in pain. Active euthanasia could allow people to die quickly, less painfully and with greater dignity.

8 Voluntary euthanasia is already allowed in other European Countries

The Netherlands, Belgium and Luxembourg allow euthanasia, so why not the UK? Supporters of euthanasia would argue that this permits people to die with dignity. Due to the fact that voluntary active euthanasia is illegal in the UK, many people who wish to die with dignity are forced to travel abroad in order to do so. This not only involves a financial cost for the family, but also adds further stress to what is already a distressing time. Legalising voluntary active euthanasia would allow people to spend their last few days in their own home environment.

9 It is not right to use the limited resources of the NHS on expensive treatment merely to prolong the life of a dying person by a few days or weeks

A hospital has a limited financial budget and artificially prolonging the life of someone who is going to die by keeping them on a life support machine is not achieving the best value for money for the hospital's many patients. It would be a better use of resources to use this money to treat other patients and to improve their chances of survival or quality of life. The money could be spent, for example, on performing a heart transplant on a young child, whose quality of life could be dramatically improved and who could go on to live for many years.

Arguments against euthanasia

There are also a number of arguments against euthanasia, including:

1 The principle of the 'sanctity of life'

This argument is often used by religious believers. It is based on the belief that human life is sacred and that, therefore, no person has the right to take his or her own life or the life of another person. If life is sacred (set apart for God's purposes) and created by Him, then only He can end it. Euthanasia therefore challenges God's will.

2 People who are a suffering a terminal illness are vulnerable

As a result of this, they should not be asked to make a definite decision whilst suffering. Their judgment might be clouded by pain. Patients might feel that they do not want to impose on their family by continuing to live and therefore feel pressurised into ending their own lives.

3 Making doctors or nurses perform euthanasia will undermine people's confidence in these professions

'Dignity in Dying' claim that there is no evidence that the patient's confidence in doctors and nurses would be jeopardised if their role were extended to include ending lives. This is not supported by evidence from either doctors or patients.

4 A mistaken diagnosis could lead to a request for euthanasia

Doctors and medical staff are only human - they can make mistakes. Even patients in a persistent vegetative state have been known to recover. Recovery from brain injury takes place at different rates, and it is only after a period of twelve months that it is diagnosed as persistent, i.e. permanent. There are, however, well-documented cases of recovery after this time, although as every month goes by the likelihood of recovery is diminished. Not every illness diagnosed as terminal will necessarily end in death. Cases of patients given a terminal prognosis, only to live significantly longer than anticipated or to recover entirely, are by no means rare.

5 How can we know the motive for an act of euthanasia?

When a person asks for death, can we be sure that the person isn't crying out in despair, rather than making a definitive decision? Can doctors be sure that patients know and understand all the facts? Any euthanasia process would have to be able to establish, beyond any doubt, the true intentions of the patient who is requesting euthanasia and that the patient is fully aware of the situation. The risk of misinformation or a failure to comprehend the situation leaves the patient vulnerable to a decision that he or she might not truly want to make.

6 The 'slippery slope' argument

The 'slippery slope' argument maintains that euthanasia is the thin end of the wedge - that once we accept euthanasia, the door is open for all sorts of other procedures and abuses, including infanticide. The argument is that euthanasia involves crossing a line and once this line is crossed the consequences are unforeseeable. If you allow euthanasia, why not allow infanticide, killing of the handicapped, etc.? There is also the danger that voluntary euthanasia could then develop into compulsory euthanasia.

7 Euthanasia is a decision which does not just affect the patient

Ultimately, voluntary euthanasia, in its physician-assisted form, isn't simply the concern of an individual. It affects others and society as a whole - the doctor who assists, the nurses who are caring for the patient, the hospital in which it takes place and the wider community. The argument of an individual's right to die must be set against the community in which individuals exist. Acceptance of the practice of killing in hospitals could reduce the respect for life that civilizations uphold now more than ever in terms of human rights.

8 Doctors have a duty to protect life

The Good Medical Practice guide for doctors (2006) issued by the General Medical Council, states that doctors are 'personally accountable for their professional practice and must always be prepared to justify their decisions and actions.' Perhaps the most enduring - certainly the most quoted - tradition in the history of medicine is the Hippocratic Oath. Named after the famous Greek physician Hippocrates, this oath was written as a guideline for the medical ethics of doctors. The oath includes several duties that a physician must perform, such as:

- the duty to never harm a patient;
- the duty to work to the best of their ability for the good of the patient;
- the duty to remain free from all intentional injustice.

Although the exact words have changed over time, the general intention is the same - to respect those who have imparted their knowledge to the science of medicine, to respect the patient, and to promise to treat them to the best of the physician's ability.

9 Death does not have to been painful – the Hospice Movement

The development of effective palliative care means that it is certainly not the case that all terminal patients will face a painful, undignified death. The hospice movement exists to care for terminal patients and to educate the public and the medical profession in alternatives to the extremes of a painful death or euthanasia. A hospice is a house or home dedicated to the care of terminally ill patients and there are over one hundred in the UK. People who have a terminal (fatal) illness can find respite care there during their illness and hopefully return home. If they cannot return home, they may go to a nursing home. A patient may well be under the care of the hospice for a long time, but most of that care will be in their own home via Macmillan Nurses (who are usually employed by the hospice) or in day care. Some are places where people will go for the final stages of their illness. The hospice movement specialises in pain control and aims to give people with painful and terminal diseases the best possible quality of life.

For reflection

Is it better morally to ease a person's pain as much as possible and ensure they continue to live or to end their pain altogether by helping them die?

Can a natural death be dignified?

An outline of religious views on euthanasia

Judaism

Arguments against euthanasia

1 Many Jews support the 'sanctity of life' argument against euthanasia. According to the Book of Genesis, God is the Creator of life. Human beings are made in God's image (Genesis 1:28) and so they deserve dignity and respect. All that God creates is good and He is the only one who should determine when it should end - life is a God-given gift.

2 God also gave humans dominion over all creation, and so we have a responsibility to use God's gifts to the full, including the gift of life (Genesis 1:26)

3 There is the religious duty in the Ten Commandments to 'Honour your father and mother' (Exodus 20:12). This is often interpreted as meaning that ending the life of an elderly relative would be wrong.

4 Jews also refer to the prohibition of 'killing' in the Ten Commandments (Exodus 20:13) – 'You shall not kill'. By allowing euthanasia we are allowing the killing of another human being.

5 The Book of Job suggests that suffering is part of God's plan and taking a life is wrong. Despite living through considerable suffering Job refuses to take his own life, arguing that we must accept suffering just as we accept happiness and joy. 'The Lord has given and the Lord has taken away.' (Job 1:21). Many Jews believe that Jewish law forbids active euthanasia and regards it as murder: for them there are no exceptions to this rule and it makes no difference if the person concerned wants to die.

Arguments in favour of euthanasia

1 The teaching of Rabbi Isserles states: 'If there is anything which causes a hindrance to the departure of the soul … then it is permissible to remove it.' In more modern language, this means that if something is an impediment to the natural process of death and the patient only survives because of it, it is permitted under Jewish law to withdraw that thing. So if a patient is certain to die, and is only being kept alive by a ventilator, it is permissible to switch off the ventilator since it is impeding the natural process of death.

2 Rabbi Moshe Feinstein and Rabbi Shlomo Zalman Auerbach have ruled that a dying patient should not be kept alive by artificial means where the treatment does not cure the illness but merely prolongs the patient's life temporarily and the patient is suffering great pain. Pain relief medicine can be given even though it may hasten death, as long as the dose is not certain to kill, and the intention is not to kill but to relieve pain (the Principle of Double Effect).

3 Some Jews may argue they are fulfilling their religious duty in the Ten Commandments to 'Honour your father and mother' (Exodus 20:12) by respecting their parent's wish to die.

4 There is also great debate on whether the sixth commandment shoud be translated from the original Hebrew text as – 'You shall not kill' or 'You shall not murder' (Exodus 20:13). Some Jews may argue that if the Hebrew word 'ratsah' is translated as 'murder' this implies that you are intentionally wanting to cause harm to another person - which is wrong, whereas when performing euthanasia you are 'killing'. When

you 'kill' in this instance you do not intentionally cause harm, but your intention is to end the suffering of another human being and therefore this is permissible.

Christianity

Arguments against euthanasia

1 Christians support the 'sanctity of life' argument against euthanasia. According to the Book of Genesis, God is the Creator of life. Human beings are made in God's image (Genesis 1:28) and so they deserve dignity and respect. All that God creates is good and He is the only one who should determine when it should end - life is a God-given gift.

2 God gave humans dominion over all creation, and so they have a responsibility to use God's gifts to the full, including the gift of life. (Genesis 1:26)

3 Christians also refer to the prohibition of 'killing' in the Ten Commandments (Exodus 20:13) – 'Do not kill'. By allowing euthanasia they are allowing the killing of another human being.

4 Despite living through considerable suffering Job refused to take his own life, arguing that we must accept suffering just as we accept happiness and joy. We are free to find meaning, even in the midst of all our troubles. Some Christians see suffering as an opportunity for spiritual growth and respond to it as Jesus did - in a positive way.

5 St Paul stated 'Do you not know that your body is a temple of the Holy Spirit' (1 Corinthians 6:19). This also implies that we should not destroy ourselves, as all life contains God's Holy Spirit.

6 In the 1995 encyclical Evangelium Vitae, Pope John Paul II confirmed earlier positions of the Roman Catholic Church: 'Euthanasia is a grave violation of the law of God, since it is the deliberate and morally unacceptable killing of a human person. This doctrine is based upon the natural law and upon the written word of God'.

7 Euthanasia also goes against one of the primary precepts of Natural Law – 'to live'. By killing someone you are preventing them from fulfilling one of their God-given purposes, which is 'to live'. A distinction is made, however, between the deliberate ending of a life and easing a person's pain through administering drugs which have the side-effect of killing the person (the Principle of Double Effect).

8 Some Christians would say that if we care for each other, offering proper support and pain relief, euthanasia should not be needed. A number of Christians work in the hospice movement which seeks to care for patients so that the 'quality of life' is maintained as death approaches. Jesus himself stated that we should show compassion to others: 'Love one another as I have loved you.' (John 13:34)

Arguments in favour of euthanasia

1 On the other hand, there are some Christians who believe that people should be allowed to die with dignity and would wish the option of legal euthanasia to be available. They argue that Jesus commanded us to show compassion - 'Love one another as I have loved you' (John 13:34) - and if this involves helping someone die, then so be it.

2 Some Christians may argue that they are fulfilling their religious duty in the Ten Commandments to 'Honour your father and mother' (Exodus 20:12) by respecting their parent's wish to die.

3   There is also great debate about whether the sixth commandment should be translated from the original Hebrew text as 'You shall not kill' or 'You shall not murder' (Exodus 20:13). Some Christians may argue that if the Hebrew word ratsah is translated as 'murder' it implies an intention to cause harm to another person - which is wrong. But performing euthanasia is 'killing' without intending to cause harm, to end the suffering of another human being - which is permissible.

4   The relevance of our 'intention' was developed by the Catholic theologian Thomas Aquinas in his Principle of Double Effect; this states that where there is a double effect, one of the effects is intended while the other is unintended. So Christians could argue that euthanasia should be allowed if your intention is not deliberately to end a life, but rather to ease someone's pain by administering drugs - which would have the side-effect of killing them.

5   There do appear to be two apparent examples of voluntary euthanasia in the Old Testament:

    a) the first is when Abimelech asks his armour bearer to kill him (Judges 9:52-5). Abimelech, believing himself to be fatally wounded in battle, asks his armour-bearer to kill him, which he does. The Israelite leader is thus spared the 'indignity' of being killed by a woman. His death is seen as just retribution for Abimelech's own murder of his seventy brothers. We are not told if the armour-bearer is punished. Some Christians could argue that if Abimelech was allowed to die with dignity then so should others be;

    b) the second example is the death of king Saul. In one account (1 Samuel 31) Saul commits suicide. In another (2 Samuel 1) an Amalekite claims to have killed Saul as a result of Saul's own request to be killed. David then orders the execution of the Amalekite because this foreigner dared to kill the king, rather than because he thought the compassionate killing of Saul constituted a capital offence (2 Samuel 1:14). So the Amalekite was killed for killing the King (God's representative) rather than for helping someone to die.

Islam

Arguments against euthanasia

1   Muslims reject the idea of euthanasia – every soul is perfect even if the body is not. 'And no person can ever die except by Allah's leave and at an appointed term.' (Surah 3:145) Life is a gift from Allah and Muslims have a duty to respect it and submit to his will. 'Destroy not yourselves. Surely Allah is ever merciful to you.' (Surah 4:29)

2   The reason for any suffering will be known to Allah. Allah is not cruel so there must be a reason for the pain. Allah decides how long a person has to live, it is not the personal choice of the individual and Allah is never unfair. 'When your time expires, you will not be able to delay the reckoning for a single hour, just as you cannot bring it forward by a single hour.' (Surah 16:61).

3   Everything has a natural shariah (a correct path or purpose given to it by Allah) so Muslims should not go against nature.

4   Muslims also have a duty to care for elderly and sick people, particularly family members – 'Treat with kindness your parents and kindred, and orphans and those in need.' (Surah 2:83).

5   The Islamic European Council for Fatwa and Research (ECFR) ruled in July 2003 that 'active' and 'passive' euthanasia or mercy killing and suicide are all forbidden in Islam.

'It is prohibited for a patient to kill him/herself or for others to kill him/her even if the patient himself allowed them to do so. The first case is nothing but suicide, while the second one is taking a life.'

The council ruled that the removal of life-support machines for the clinically dead is permissible:

'These machines help patients breathe and activate their blood cycle, but if they are already clinically dead and have lost all their senses due to brain damage, it makes no sense to keep these machines running, because they cost the hospital a lot of money and might be direly needed by other patients,' the council said.

Hinduism

Arguments against euthanasia

1   Hindus believe that all life is sacred. They believe that a terminally ill individual has to wait for God to decide when they will die.

2   Euthanasia would interfere with a person's dharma (duty) and cause the soul and the body to be separated at an inappropriate time.

3   Suffering is caused by karma from a previous life, so it must therefore be endured in order to eventually achieve moksha (release from reincarnation). Whoever helped someone to die would also be causing bad karma for themselves.

4   Another important principle in Hinduism is ahimsa - not being violent or causing harm to other beings, so this would also seem to forbid euthanasia. Hindus believe that a person must be cared for until they die.

Arguments in favour of euthanasia

1   Gandhi, on the other hand, argued that ahimsa might permit killing if it was founded on a totally selfless motive in order to bring about spiritual benefit. It could therefore be argued that by helping to end a painful life a person is performing a good deed and so fulfilling their moral obligations.

2   Hindus could also argue that keeping a person artificially alive on a life-support machine, rather than helping to end their life, would also be a bad deed because not wanting to lose a loved one is a selfish reason.

Buddhism

Arguments against euthanasia

1   Buddhists do not have one view of euthanasia, but many Buddhists follow a moral code called the Ten Precepts. These are not rules, but rather promises that a person should live up to which will help them to develop spiritually. One of the precepts states that we should not 'harm any living creature'. This is understood in the very wide sense of killing or hurting - not only physically but also mentally and emotionally. This precept would suggest that committing euthanasia is therefore wrong.

2   Members of the monastic sangha would be expelled if they encouraged someone to help another person to commit voluntary euthanasia or if they themselves helped an

individual to commit voluntary euthanasia. They are not allowed to deliberately kill a person or incite someone else to kill a person. Metta (love) and karuna (compassion) form the basis of their teachings.

3   There are a number of Buddhist hospices. Death is not an escape from suffering because a person's karma continues into their next existence. The Buddhist Hospice Trust offers help and support for the dying and their friends and relatives. They do not offer medical or nursing care, but focus on catering for spiritual needs.

4   Dukkha (suffering) is seen as a natural part of life. Dying is seen as an opportunity for spiritual growth and should not be interfered with.

5   Other Buddhists would question the intention of anyone arguing for euthanasia – is it seen as an act of compassion or abdication of responsibility for another person? The Venerable Thich Nhat Hahn said 'Let us fill our hearts with our own compassion – towards ourselves and towards all living beings. Let us pray that we cease to be the cause of suffering to each other. Let us plead with ourselves to live in a way which will not deprive other beings of air, water, food, shelter or the chance to live.'

Arguments in favour of euthanasia

1   The Dalai Lama has stated that 'In the event a person is definitely going to die and he is either in great pain or has virtually become a vegetable, and prolonging his existence is only going to cause difficulties and suffering for others, the termination of his life may be permitted according to Mahayana Buddhist ethics.' (Letter by the Dalai Lama, *Asia Week*, November 1985).

2   Kalu Rinpoche, in '*The Tibetan book of living and dying*', said clearly both that people who are terminally ill and decide to take themselves off life-support perform a 'karmically neutral act', and that assisting a dying person who asks us to remove life-support is also karmically neutral, provided our basic motivation is to relieve the patient's suffering. Some Buddhists may indeed oppose euthanasia, but there is no general Buddhist consensus on this issue, particularly in the Mahayana traditions.

Sikhism

Arguments against euthanasia

1   Sikhs also see life as a God-given gift. Many Sikhs are against euthanasia as they believe it is up to God to decide when we die: 'Whatever God does, accept that with pleasure; in comfort and in suffering, meditate on Him.' (AG 209, SGGS)

2   Sikhs believe that human beings should accept that suffering occurs and try to make the best of it in order to improve their karma.

3   A great deal of Sikh teaching is devoted to the care of others and by providing such good care for those suffering (e.g. in a hospice) they hope that the person will not want to end their life.

Arguments in favour of euthanasia

1   However there is not a single Sikh approach to this issue. Some believe that life is a gift from God, but Sikhism also teaches that we have a duty to use life in a responsible way. A number of Sikhs believe it is the quality of life that matters, not the length. Sikhs should not be afraid of death – it is not the end.

'The dawn of a new day is the herald of the sunset. Earth is not thy permanent home. Life is like a shadow on the wall. All thy friends have departed. Thou must go soon.' (Ravidas AG 793)

2 Sikhs contemplating euthanasia for themselves or others should make the appropriate distinction between ending life, and not artificially prolonging a terminal state.

3 Voluntary euthanasia would be acceptable to some, so long as there were medical/legal safeguards in place.

Task

Writing task	a) Explain why one major world religion might oppose the legalisation of Euthanasia.
	b) 'Helping someone to die who wants to die cannot be wrong.' Assess this view.

Glossary

active euthanasia	To deliberately take action designed to end a patient's life
euthanasia	Literally 'a good death' - a medical procedure by which a person terminates his or her own life because of extreme pain or suffering, or by which the life of another person is either allowed to come to an end or is brought to an end, with legal consent, because of a critical medical condition
non-voluntary euthanasia	The killing of a patient who is not able to express their wishes about whether they should live or die
passive euthanasia	To allow a patient to die by withdrawing medical treatment or nourishment, for example turning off a life-support system to which a patient in a coma has been connected
principle of 'double effect'	When a person who performs an action in order to achieve a good primary effect (consequence) is not held responsible for any un-intentional secondary effects
quality of life	A human condition in which a person enjoys a degree of physical, intellectual and emotional well-being, the absence of which through severe illness is sometimes used as an argument in favour of euthanasia
sanctity of life	A belief that human life is sacred and that, therefore, no person has the right to take his or her own life or the life of another person
voluntary euthanasia	To cause a patient's death, where consent has been given by the individual concerned

Animal Rights

Aim

After studying this chapter, you should be able to show a clear knowledge and understanding of the differing views on the moral status of animals and some of the arguments given both for and against the use of animals for food, experimentation, hunting/culling and as pets/entertainment. You should also be able to understand the contrasting arguments given for killing animals for food, for pleasure or for medical research and be able to determine to what extent animal rights are compatible with religious principles.

Do you agree with Aristotle's view of animal rights?

Do animals have a moral status?

Historical background

For centuries, many humans in the Western world have generally adopted the stance taken by the Greek philosopher Aristotle that animals existed simply to fulfil human desires and needs. He said that animals, unlike humans, did not have the ability to reason, and as a result animals had no moral status. This meant they had no value in themselves and that they did not deserve to be given any 'rights'. Such views were still in existence in the 17th Century - Descartes stated 'I think therefore I am', implying that the ability to reason was a key characteristic of moral status.

There was a time, in Western thought at least, when animals were simply considered a resource for us to use and enjoy, but there is now far more concern about the suffering inflicted by humans on animals. The issue of the welfare of animals, often refered to as 'animal rights', has become significant, particularly within Western society.

Seminar topic

If you accept as a starting point Aristotle's view that animals lack the ability of rational thought, how else do animals differ from humans?

Our scientific knowledge and understanding of animals has increased significantly in recent centuries. Developments such as Darwin's theory of evolution have caused people to rethink the so-called 'gap' between humans and animals. If we share a common link with other animals such as primates, this calls into question claims that we are superior to other species. Recent research has found that apes share almost 99 per cent of their functional genes with humans, and even when differences in less significant DNA are taken into account they remain 96 per cent identical.

Many religious believers have also begun to re-examine the importance of humankind's role in the world. Christians have, in modern times, stressed the need for us to demonstrate responsible **stewardship** of the world. This is based on the idea that we have been given the responsibility by God to care for the world, its environment and the other species found in it.

Which if any of these approaches do you take to the issue of animal rights?

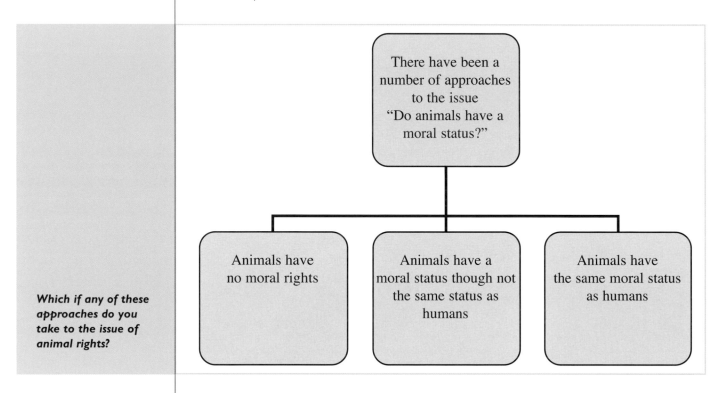

Task

Writing task	Write a sentence on your view of the moral status of animals. Compare your answer with another member of your group.

I *Animals have no moral rights – we have no moral obligations to animals.*

This means that animals have only an instrumental value – they have value only because they are useful to humans. For example, humans need to eat meat, therefore killing animals for meat is simply part of our biological existence. Animals have no moral status or rights, because they do not appear to have the ability to reason and do not possess free will or a conscience. Animals do not appear to have the capacity to act 'morally'. For example they cannot think rationally about whether to kill or not, they simply act instinctively. Some would argue that rights are appropriate only for beings that have self-awareness and a social system, and can express their desires and be held accountable for their actions – which animals cannot.

2 *Animals have a moral status – we should treat them with respect, but ultimately they are of less moral worth than humans.*

This implies that animals have an intrinsic value – they are worthy in themselves of a moral status. Animals are not equal to us (for the reasons outlined above): as full members of the moral community humans have rights and duties, whereas animals do not. For example, if you have the right to live, then everyone has the right not to be killed. However animals are unable to understand this concept and so therefore do not deserve rights. Another argument is that humans, as the most powerful and superior species, have a responsibility to care for the other species. The idea of animals having a moral status is also often linked to the issue of animals experiencing pain and suffering. If they can experience pain and suffering then should they not be afforded rights? Do they not deserve the right to be treated with respect? We should also consider the fact that if we mistreat animals we cannot claim to have greater moral worth as human beings.

3 *Animals have the same moral status as humans. They deserve the same respect as other species such as humans.*

This claims that animals have equal intrinsic value – all beings have equal value in themselves for what they are. Animals deserve the same rights as those given to humans. All beings have an inherent value and possess it equally. We are wrong to view animals as a resource to be killed for sport, experimented on or used for fashion. The idea that animals have a significant moral status has been developed by philosophers such as Richard Ryder and Peter Singer. Ryder used the term 'speciesism' to describe 'the unjust belief that one species is superior to another'. This means that a member of one species has a clear prejudice against members of another species. Singer believes that, just like racism, this attitude is wrong. He believes that if animals have rights, then this must include the right to be regarded as just as valuable as any other species, even humans.

Task

Research task	Use the BBC Religion & Ethics website (www.bbc.co.uk/religion/ethics/animals/ see the 'Using animals' section) to identify three aspects of animal rights.
	What are the ethical issues raised by these three aspects? Are there any moral differences about the way the animals are being used? Is one form more acceptable than the others? If so, why?

The attitude we adopt to the moral status of animals will ultimately affect our view of the various animal rights issues. Take, for example, the issue of humans being allowed to destroy the natural habitats of animals (such as the Amazon rainforest): many people may support the view that animals have no moral status and that if we are superior to animals then we should be allowed to clear rainforests to grow crops for an increasing human population, or to use the timber for construction. Our needs take priority over the needs of any animals. However, if you take the view that animals have some rights, or equal rights to humans, you may argue that we have no right to clear rainforests, because we will be destroying the natural environment for these animals. Also some species may even become extinct as result of this deforestation: what right do humans have to wipe out an entire species of animal forever?

Do our increasing needs warrant the destruction of animals' natural habitats?

Issues involving the use of animals

We will now go on to look at a number of issues in greater detail. The moral debate about animal rights tends to centre around topics such as:

- Animals as food

- Animal experimentation

- Bloodsports / hunting

- Culling

- Animals as pets / entertainment.

The views that different people take on these issues are generally determined by their view on the moral status of animals, as we have seen.

i. Animals as food

It is estimated that about 90-95% of the animals that suffer and die due to human intervention do so because of the demand for animals as 'food'. Approximately 2.5 million animals are killed for food per day in the UK. Genetic modification of some of these animals can also lead to higher meat yields. This raises the further issue that even if it is acceptable to breed animals for food, is it also acceptable to deliberately genetically modify them in order to make more money? What could be the side effects to the animals of such intervention? How could eating such food affect humans in the long term?

'Intensive', 'industrialised', 'factory' – these are all terms that can be used to describe modern farming methods: 'intensive' because as many animals as possible are placed together in the smallest legally allowable space; 'industrialised' because there are often automatic means of feeding, watering and waste clearing; 'factory' because the philosophy behind this type of farming is mass production – to make as much money as possible.

One form of factory farming involves battery hens. 93% of eggs in the European Union come from battery hens and 70% of Britain's eggs. Twenty-four million chickens are currently battery farmed in Britain, ensuring the low price of eggs and chicken products. On such farms five hens are packed into a cage of only 45cm x 50cm, where they cannot perform basic functions such as spreading their wings, perching or making a nest, or even walking or running.

Cages are stacked into windowless sheds, with artificial lighting for about 17 hours a day to promote egg laying. As an egg is laid, it rolls onto a conveyor belt and is taken away to be boxed. The birds are placed in these cages at about 18 weeks old and are not removed until they are 18 months to two years old, when they are killed. Slaughtered battery hens are processed into soups, baby foods, stock cubes, school dinners, or used in the restaurant trade. In 1999 the European Union passed a law banning battery cages from 2012, after which hens will have to be housed in bigger cages, with nests and perches.

Another form of factory farming involves the artificial insemination of cattle. This is a routine procedure on dairy farms and the vast majority of dairy cattle are produced in this way. In order to produce commercial quantities of milk, dairy cows are routinely made pregnant by artificial insemination, as this increases the amount of milk they produce. Calves are usually removed from their mothers within 24 hours of birth, after suckling their mother's first antibody-rich milk, known as colostrum. Separation of mother and infant causes anxiety and suffering for both animals. Dairy cows are usually kept outside on pasture for the summer months, but during the rest of the year they are kept indoors, typically in concrete cubicle houses. Each cow has a cubicle to stand or lie in and behind each animal a passageway collects the animal's waste. However, many cubicles still in use were designed years ago and have become too small for the modern, larger animal. This has also resulted in cows standing in the dunging passageway, which is a major health concern.

As a result of this and other animal rights issues, some people choose to become vegetarians. They believe, for religious or other reasons, that it is unethical to kill animals for food, so they choose a diet that does not involve eating animals. Others go even further and become vegans, refusing to eat, drink or use any substances derived from animals (e.g. milk, fish, meat, eggs, cheese and leather).

For reflection

Is factory farming a justifiable method of food production?

Arguments in favour of killing animals for food include:

1 **As superior beings we have the right to do what we like with animals.** If we have 'dominion' over animals we can use them for anything as we see fit, including for food.

2 **Using animals is necessary - we need food to live.** Food is a basic necessity for survival, meat is a source of food, therefore we eat meat to survive.

3 **Many animals today are created for food: they would not exist if we did not create them.** Animals such as pigs, cows, chickens, etc. are bred specifically to be killed for meat. If they were not needed for meat then they would not have been created through breeding in the first place.

4 **Humans killing animals for food is part of the 'natural' order.** Animals kill other animals for food and in turn we kill animals for food. This is simply part of the natural 'food chain' in action.

Arguments against killing animals for food include:

1 **If animals have rights then surely they deserve the most basic right - the right to life.** Unless you believe animals have no rights, then you must recognise that they have some rights. If they have some rights then surely they deserve the most basic right of all – the right to life.

2 **Humans do not need to eat meat to survive.** Vegetarians/vegans would say you do not need meat to survive and that in fact you can have a healthier lifestyle if you do not eat meat.

3 **Many of the animals reared by factory farming live in poor conditions.** This shows a lack of respect for their treatment. For example, pigs can often be kept in the dark to keep them calm, and can become distressed when brought into the light when transported for slaughter.

4 **Animals killed for food are often killed in brutal ways** e.g. shooting, electrocution, slitting the blood vessels in the neck, etc. If animals do have a moral status, and therefore rights, they deserve the right not to be killed for food in these ways.

An Oncomouse is bred specifically for cancer research. Is this fair?

ii. Animals in medical and non-medical experimentation

More than 2 million animal experiments take place every year in the UK. For example, the OncoMouse is a genetically modified laboratory mouse used to carry a specific gene called an activated oncogene. This gene increases the mouse's susceptibility to cancer, and thus makes the mouse suitable for cancer research. In order to justify (or not) such actions it may be helpful to ask the following questions about the experimentation:

1   What is the reason for the experiment?

Many would argue that it is easier to justify experiments if they are used, for example, to test a cure for a serious disease, rather than for a new beauty product. It is argued that experimenting on animals to save human lives brings greater benefit to us in the long term than testing a shampoo that makes your hair shine. Those who claim we have no moral obligation towards animals might disagree, however, and allow experimentation for any reason.

2   Which animals are being used?

People tend to oppose experimentation on animals to which we have the greatest emotional attachment, such as primates or popular pets (e.g. rabbits, dogs and cats). However the majority of experiments are carried out on mice/rats. This raises another issue, however: should one animal receive a higher moral status than another?

3   How much pain is being caused to the animal?

In *An Introduction to the Principles of Morals and Legislation*, the Utilitarian Jeremy Bentham said about animal rights: 'The question is not, can they reason? Nor, can they talk? But, can they suffer?' Clearly animals can experience pain and suffering (some, it appears, more than others). If this is true, do we not have an obligation to minimise this suffering?

Arguments in favour of animal experiments include:

1   **Human life has greater intrinsic value than animal life.** If a human life is worth more than an animal life, then an animal life can be taken in order to save a human life.

2   **The information gained from such experiments could not be gained in other ways.** Some would claim that other ways of testing medicines, such as computer modelling, does not produce results as accurate as testing on animals.

3   **The pain inflicted on the animals is minimised and controlled by legislation.** There are strict laws in place governing the use of animals in medicine, which prevents unnecessary suffering.

4   **Useful medicines have been developed as a result of animal experimentation such as vaccines against rabies, polio, TB, etc.** Without such experimentation we might still be trying to develop these medicines.

Arguments against animal experiments include:

1   **Animals have as much a right to life as human beings.** If the animals are used because they are biologically close enough to humans, then what right do we have to use them for testing? Surely they have the same rights as us if they are biologically so similar?

2   **The experiments cause unnecessary suffering to animals and degrade us as human beings.** If animals can feel pain then why should we cause them to suffer when there are others ways to test these medicines (see below). Also, even if we have been given dominion over the animals, we should use that power in a positive way to care for animals and not to inflict suffering. If we cause deliberate suffering to animals that must mean we have abused the power we have been given.

3   **The benefits (if any) of such experiments could be gained in other ways** e.g. computer modelling – using technology combined with current knowledge to predict what effects and side effects the drug will cause.

4   **The stress endured by animals in the laboratory can render the results meaningless.** Animals who are not in their natural environment (such as in a laboratory) may become stressed, which will mean any results gained from experimenting on them will be not be accurate.

Scientists are being encouraged to:

reduce   (the number of animals used);

refine   (each experiment so that the pain and suffering is kept to a minimum);

replace   (find alternative methods of research to animal experimentation).

However, if we stopped animal testing altogether would this stop progress towards curing potentially fatal infections or diseases such as HIV or cancer?

Seminar topic

Banning animal experimentation may slow down any progress made by medical science towards finding a cure for serious human diseases. Is such a move justifiable?

iii. Bloodsports / hunting

The term 'blood sport' is used to describe a sport that involves causing suffering to animals. There are many forms of blood sports such as bull fighting, dog fighting, badger baiting and hunting. Badger baiting, for example, was outlawed in 1835, but still continues as an illegal blood 'sport'. Badgers are dug from their setts and either forced to fight against dogs on the spot, or taken away for fights to be staged elsewhere. A number of dogs will often be set against a badger. The badger may have already been partially disabled by someone to 'even up' the fight. Both dogs and badger sustain terrible injuries, with the badger killed either by the dogs or by the humans involved. The police were given greater powers to prosecute those involved in this form of animal cruelty by the 1992 Protection of Badgers Act.

Hunting is also a long-standing human activity and can take place either for food or for sport. In recent times more and more people have questioned the validity of hunting, particularly as a sport, as our understanding of animals has developed. For example 'hunting with hounds' was outlawed in the UK in November 2004.

Arguments in favour of hunting include:

1   **Some animals are a nuisance to other animals, so they are hunted to prevent a loss of stock.** Farmers claim, for example, that foxes kill their livestock so they have a right to kill them to protect the stock.

Do you think that hunting with hounds should be illegal?

Why? / Why not?

2 **Hunting is a tradition, an ancient sport, and should therefore be maintained.** Those who support hunting would argue that it is part of our cultural heritage and we therefore have a duty to maintain it.

3 **Skilled hunters ensure the animals do not suffer unnecessarily.** Expert hunters know how to kill an animal as painlessly as possible and cause minimal suffering to the animal.

4 **People need to eat and in some parts of the world, hunting is the main source of food.** There are places in the world where hunting still provides necessary dietary requirements or supplements.

Arguments against hunting include:

1 **There must be more humane ways of killing the animals, if they do have to be killed.** If an animal has to be killed because it has been killing livestock, then it should be killed in the least painful way e.g. by being shot, rather than being hunted for hours and becoming stressed first.

2 **Hunting one species can disrupt the food chain for another species.** If you hunt one species of animal to extinction, or even to near extinction, this disrupts the food chain for animals which hunt it.

3 **The 'tradition' argument is a poor one** – slavery was also traditional, but that does not mean it was right.

4 **Organised hunts can do greater damage to the countryside than the animal being hunted.** The people, dogs, horses etc. involved in a hunt cause greater environmental damage to the land than the animal they are hunting. What about the pollution caused by those driving to an arranged hunt, for example?

Seminar topic

Is hunting a valid pursuit or does it degrade humanity?

iv. Culling

One method of controlling numbers of animals has been through 'culling' or population control. For example, in February 2008 the South African government announced that it was going to authorise an elephant cull for the first time in thirteen years. People living close to the elephants had complained that elephants were dangerous, ate crops and competed with people for water.

Also in April 2008, the Welsh Assembly Government announced a 'targeted cull' of badgers as part of a plan to eradicate the spread of tuberculosis (TB) in cattle. It would probably take place in south-west Wales or a county bordering England where TB was worst, although the specific area, culling method or length of cull had yet to be decided. Farmers have long blamed badgers for spreading bovine TB and want a widespread cull, but animal groups say evidence does not support this. There has been limited badger culling before, but it is the first time in Britain that such a wide-scale measure, within a defined area, has been used as an attempt to control the disease.

Arguments in favour of culling include:

1 **Culling prevents potential damage to livestock or infections** e.g. badger culls to prevent the spread of TB.

2 **It restores 'balance' if one species is killing off a native species.** It is better to intervene to prevent 'natural selection' making some species extinct, by reducing the number of the 'aggressive' species.

3 **Culling prevents the loss of food sources for other animals or humans.** If one species is consuming the majority of the resources (e.g. water) needed for other species or humans to survive, then it needs to be culled in order to prevent this from happening.

4 **Culling removes animals which pose a threat to human life.** For example, one of the reasons given for the cull of elephants in South Africa was the danger posed to human life by herds of elephants.

Arguments against culling include:

1 **We often cull for financial reasons, which is a misuse of our dominion over animals.** For example, some countries earn millions of pounds from selling the meat and fur produced as a result of culling.

2 **We have no right to interfere with nature** – if one species is becoming extinct we have no right to stop this.

3 **There is often an alternative to culling** e.g. using noise devices to deter seals from damaging fishermen's nets.

4 **Methods used to cull animals are often brutal,** for example some seals are killed with a 'hakapik', a 4 or 5 foot wooden pole with a bent, metal spike fixed to the end. Those performing the cull aim a blow directly at the seal pup's head.

5 **Culling is not effective in the long term as the species will eventually repopulate the area.** Over time the population of the culled species will return back to its original numbers.

v. Animals as pets or entertainment

For millions of people the closest relationship they have with an animal is with their pet. Whilst the majority of pet owners use their dominion (control) over animals in a responsible way and care for them, sadly some do not. RSPCA statistics show that in the UK in 2006 nearly 900 people were convicted of cruelty to their pets.

Arguments in favour of keeping animals as pets include:

1 **Many animals receive better treatment as pets than they would do in the wild.** They are regularly provided with food, water, shelter and affection which they may not get in the wild.

2 **We can learn about animal behaviour from spending time with our pets.** If you spend a lot of time with a species you can often learn a lot about animal behaviour.

3 **Having a pet may encourage people to behave responsibly towards other animals.** By having a pet you may come to realise that having 'dominion' over an animal brings the responsibility to care for it.

4 **Such relationships allow expressions of emotion, companionship and shared enjoyment** e.g. a dog owner walking their dog.

Are we being cruel by keeping animals as pets?

Arguments against keeping animals as pets include:

1   **We have no right to keep an animal in captivity in order to learn from it.** Keeping an animal away from its natural habitat is cruel and can cause the animal undue stress.

2   **We often abandon pets when they cost us money or are no longer cute or fashionable.** In 2005, 6,500 pets were left with the RSPCA; by 2007 this figure had increased to 9,500.

3   **The animal fails to live in its natural environment and so lives in a 'false' way.** To remove an animal from its natural environment will hinder its natural development. Does a caged parrot develop as it would normally do in the wild?

4   **If animals have rights do they not deserve the right to freedom?** If you adopt the position that animals should have some rights, or even the same rights as humans, then surely a fundamental right is that of freedom – the right to choose where they live and what they do.

vi. Animals as entertainment

Many people have at one time or other visited a zoo or circus and in doing so have used animals as a form of entertainment. There are currently four circuses in the UK that use non-domesticated animals in their acts. Such a use provokes a variety of responses. Many argue that using animals for entertainment shows a lack of respect for the animals involved, and a lack of compassion for the neglect some of these animals may suffer. However, there are several laws in place protecting the rights of such animals. For example, with regards to circus animals:

'The welfare of performing animals is provided for in the Animal Welfare Act 2006, to avoid suffering and to ensure welfare. This act prevents unnecessary cruelty or suffering to any vertebrate animal. In addition, it introduced a new 'duty of care' for any animal under the control of man, which makes owners and keepers responsible for ensuring that the welfare needs of their animals are met. This duty applies to animals kept in circuses just as to pets, farmed animals and other domestic and companion animals.

The five welfare requirements include the need:
- *for a suitable environment (place to live);*
- *for a suitable diet;*
- *to exhibit normal behaviour patterns;*
- *to be housed with, or apart from, other animals (if applicable);*
- *to be protected from pain, injury, suffering and disease.'*

(Information adapted from the Department for Environment, Food and Rural Affairs' (DEFRA) website)

Trainers and exhibitors of performing animals have to be registered with the local authority. The police, and officers of local authorities, including a vet, then have the power to enter their premises. If cruelty and neglect is detected, magistrates' courts can prohibit or restrict the training or exhibition of the animals and suspend or cancel the registration.

In March 2006 the government also announced that it intends in the future to ban the use, in travelling circuses, of certain non-domesticated species whose welfare needs cannot be satisfactorily met in that environment. 'Non-domesticted' is defined as:

'a member of a species not normally domesticated in the British Islands; a species whose collective behaviour, life cycle or physiology remains unaltered from the wild type, despite their breeding and living conditions being under human control for multiple generations.'

Arguments in favour of using animals in circuses include:

1 **Circuses help to preserve endangered species.** Circuses help to increase the numbers of animals such as tigers and elephants, which will help to prevent them from becoming extinct.

2 **They raise awareness of the animals.** By experiencing the beauty of an animal such as a lion in real life we are more likely to support campaigns to improve their welfare.

3 **As the 'superior' species we can use animals in any way we see fit.** If animals have no moral status or less moral status than humans, then we can use them as we see fit, including simply for our own amusement.

4 **The animals can live in a 'safe' environment.** Animals kept in a circus live in an environment where they are not going to be attacked by predators. They are therefore actually safer in a circus than in the wild.

Arguments against using animals for circuses include:

1 **Animals bred in captivity often cannot be returned to the wild, as they are not able to survive.** Once bred and reared in captivity, animals may lose the natural instincts needed to survive e.g. to react to danger signs, to hunt for food, etc.

2 **We have no right to remove animals from their natural habitat.** If we remove an animal from its natural habitat we effectively change its diet and its learning development and, unless we believe animals have no moral status, what right do we have to do this?

3 **Animals are still kept in 'prison'-like environments.** Circus animals are often kept in small enclosures or cages for logistical reasons e.g. ease of transportation, which is cruel and unfair on the animals involved.

4 **People are more likely to consider animals as inferior species if we allow their use for entertainment.** If animals are used simply as a means of entertainment humans are more likely to see them as having little or no moral worth and, as a result, treat them poorly when they come into contact with them

Arguments for keeping animals in zoos include:

1 **Zoos help to preserve endangered species.** They help to increase the numbers of animals such as pandas and elephants, which will help to prevent them from becoming extinct. For example, in March 2008 Australian zoos joined together with other zoos around the world to develop a conservation strategy for frogs in the 'Year of the Frog 2008'. This included protecting and breeding frogs that were on the verge of extinction.

2   **Most zoo animals are bred in captivity and not taken from the wild.** As a result of this, returning them to the wild would also not be 'natural' for those animals. They would not possess the skills to survive in the wild.

3   **Some creatures bred in captivity are released back to the wild.** This helps to increase the population of this species in the wild.

4   **Zoos are replacing poor living conditions with spacious enclosures.** To claim the animals are not being cared for would be unfair.

5   **We can learn about animal behaviour.** If you observe a particular species carefully you can often learn a lot about animal behaviour generally.

6   **Zoos help to educate people about conservation.** People can learn why many of these animals are endangered and may be more inclined to help to save them.

Arguments against keeping animals in zoos include:

1   **Only a small percentage of animals kept in zoos are endangered.** To claim this as the reason why zoos exist is therefore inaccurate.

2   **Animals should not be kept in zoos simply for our entertainment.** We do not have the right (if animals are worthy of some status or the same status as humans) to keep them locked up for our amusement; they deserve to be treated with dignity.

3   **A zoo is not appropriate for studying animal behaviour.** Animals kept in a zoo will not behave as animals would do in the wild, so studying them in a zoo gives us inaccurate information.

4   **Cramped enclosures mean that many of the animals suffer.** Not all zoos allow animals the space or type of environment they deserve.

5   **Animals bred in captivity often cannot be returned to the wild, as they are not able to survive in the wild.** Once bred and reared in captivity, animals may lose the natural instincts needed to survive e.g. to react to danger signs, to hunt for food, etc.

6   **In the modern world people can be educated about animals by using 'virtual' online zoos.** We could store the information we already hold on these animals on websites, which anyone can access use without having to keep animals in captivity.

An outline of religious views of animal rights
Judaism
Arguments against the use of animals

1   Jews derive their views on the treatment of animals from the creation story found in Genesis, where humans are given both control over, and responsibility for, animals.

2   Passages such as Deuteronomy 25:5 *'Do not muzzle your ox when it is treading out the corn'*, do seem to imply that humans should be concerned with an animal's welfare.

3   *'And the name that Adam gave to each living being has remained its name forever'* (Genesis 2:19). In Kabbalistic [Jewish mystic] teaching, as Adam named all of God's creatures, he helped define their essence. Adam swore to live in harmony with those whom he had named. Thus, at the very beginning of time, man accepted responsibility before God for all of creation. (The Jewish Declaration on Nature)

4 Hunting and killing animals for sport is not allowed, as it goes against the Schechitah rituals for kosher food.

Arguments in favour of the use of animals

Animals can be killed for food. Any animals slaughtered for food have to be killed quickly, painlessly, deliberately and individually, according to the Schechitah ritual for kosher food. The animal's throat is cut with a very sharp knife across the jugular vein so that it loses consciousness quickly.

Christianity

Arguments against the use of animals

1   In modern times Christians tend to emphasise that the world is not an accident and that everything has a purpose given to it by God. This purpose includes stewardship of the world they believe God created for them. In Genesis (1:28), humans were given dominion over the animals and the responsibility for their welfare.

2   The Rev. Andrew Linzey, an Anglican theologian and director of the Oxford Centre for Animal Ethics, supports this view. In an article in Tom Regan's book *Animal Sacrifices: Religious Perspectives on the Use of Animals in Science* he says:

    'The doctrine of creation does will not allow us unrestricted and unrestrained use of the animal world for human purposes ... We need to remind ourselves that in theological terms man's use of animals has the nature of trust; we are accountable to God. Animals do not belong to us.'

3   Whilst there is no evidence in the Gospels that Jesus was himself a vegetarian, some Christians have claimed that the creation story implies that they should be vegetarian or even vegan in response to modern factory farming methods.

4   A number of Christians have campaigned for animal rights: St Francis of Assisi, for example, was famous for his love of animals. He is known as the patron saint of animals, birds, and the environment, and it is customary for Catholic churches to hold ceremonies honouring animals around his feast day in October.

5   Other passages suggest that God values animal life – *'Are not five sparrows sold for a penny? Yet not one of them is forgotten by God'* (Luke 16:6)

6   Albert Schweitzer (1875-1965) argued in his book *Civilization and Ethics* that all life is sacred (or holy), meaning animals too. He argued that humans, animals and plants were created by God and to injure or kill any living thing on purpose is to act against God's creation.

Arguments in favour of the use of animals

1   Initially, Christianity appeared to adopt a somewhat negative approach to animal rights. St Augustine, for example, argued that animals essentially existed for the benefit of humans. As animals do not possess the ability to reason they are under the control of humans who do have this ability.

2   Thomas Aquinas (1224-1274) argued that animals exist simply for humans to use as they see fit. In his work *Summa Contra Gentiles* (c. 1260) he stated that the cruel treatment of animals is only wrong because it usually leads us to treating other humans badly as well.

3 Karl Barth (1886-1968) responded to Schweitzer's argument by stating that as God became man in the human form of Jesus, humans are the superior species. Animals cannot therefore be equal to humans.

Islam

Arguments against the use of animals

1 Muslims believe animals are made by God and therefore their care is important. They are to be treated with kindness and compassion:

    'Whoever is kind to the creatures of God is kind to himself.' (Hadith)

    'Allah has made you custodians and inheritors of the earth.' (Qur'an Surah 6 :165)

2 There are three concepts which are central to the Muslim treatment of animals: Tawhid (we were all created by God); Khalifa (we are guardians of God's creation); and Akra (we will be held accountable by God for our treatment of animals on the Day of Judgment).

3 Muslims do not allow the killing of animals for sport or fashion, or agree with keeping animals in zoos and circuses for entertainment. The Qur'an teaches that Allah expects humans to treat animals with compassion: *'There is not an animal that lives on the earth, nor a being that flies that is not part of a community like you.'* (Surah 6 : 38)

4 Muhammad told many stories which demonstrated his care for animals. He once said *'One who kills even a sparrow or anything smaller without a justifiable reason will be answerable to Allah.'* When asked what would be a justifiable reason, he stated *'to kill it for food'.* (Reported by Ahmad and Al-Nassa'i, Muslim Education Trust). To kill an animal for any other reason would therefore not be right.

5 Muhammad said that animals should not be killed without a just cause, such as for food. Animals are sacrificed in Muslim festivals such as Id al Adha and festival foods include meat. Any animal killed for food should be killed according to the Halal (permissible) method – kindly and quickly. If possible the animal should be calm and its throat cut with a very sharp knife across the jugular vein, so that it loses consciousness quickly. Prayers are said whilst this is done.

Arguments in favour of the use of animals

1 Even Muhammad said that animals could be killed for a just cause, such as for food (see above).

2 Animals are sacrificed in Muslim festivals such as Id al Adha and festival foods include meat.

3 Any animals killed for food are killed according to the Halal (permissible) method – kindly and quickly. If possible the animal should be calm and its throat then cut with a very sharp knife across the jugular vein so that it loses consciousness quickly. Prayers are said whilst this is done.

4 Muslims allow the use of animals for medical experimentation if there are no possible alternative methods. This suggests that animal life is considered to be inferior to human life.

Sikhism

Arguments against the use of animals

1 Sikhs care about and respect animals, because God created them. Sikhs consider causing willful suffering to others as wrong:

> *'God is the destroyer,*
> *preserver and creator,*
> *God is the Goddess too.*
> *Words to describe are hard to find,*
> *I would venture if I knew.'*
> *This alone my teacher taught,*
> *There is but one Lord of all creation,*
> *Forget Him not.* (Japji 5)

2 Some Sikhs are vegetarian because they believe the 'one spirit' (God) lives in all creatures. Sikhs leave the decision of becoming vegetarian or not to the individual's conscience.

3 Food given at the Langar is always vegetarian so that anyone can receive it. Guru Nanak said that 'All food is pure; for God has provided it for our sustenance' (Guru Granth Sahib: 472).

Arguments in favour of the use of animals

There is evidence of hunting within Sikh history – Guru Gobind Singh was known to hunt, although in general Sikhs consider causing wilful suffering to others as wrong.

Hinduism

Arguments against the use of animals

1 Hindus believe that all creation is interdependent and they believe in Ahimsa (non-violence).

2 The Laws of Manu also state that animals should be protected. Hindus believe that all life was created by God so they can express their love for God through their love for living beings.

   'He who hates no creature, who is friendly and compassionate to all ... he my devotee is dear to me.' (Bhagavad Gita 12:3-14)

3 Hindus believe Brahman (God) is everywhere in all things. Many of the Hindu gods appear as animals e.g. Hanuman, Ganesh, etc.

4 Hindus demonstrate reverence for the cow and most Hindus will not eat beef or beef products. The cow symbolises the special care that exists between all humans and animals. Mahatma Gandhi said

   'In its finer or spiritual sense, the term 'cow-protection' means the protection of every living creature.'

5 Many Hindus are vegetarian, but such a choice is considered to be a personal preference.

6 All animals are bound up to samsara (rebirth) so respect is shown to all animals.

   'When a man sees that the God in himself is the same God in all that is, he hurts himself by hurting others. Then he goes, indeed, to the highest path.'
   Bhagavad Gita 13v28-29.

Arguments in favour of the use of animals

1   Ancient Vedic texts such as the Rigveda make reference to animal sacrifices being made to Gods and Goddesses. In a reference to the sacrifice of a goat it says (1.162.2)

    'The dappled goat goes straight to heaven, bleating to the place dear to Indra and to Pusan.'

2   The Yajur Veda contains many more clear references to animal sacrifices, mainly in association with the full moon rite, the Soma sacrifice and its supplement. There is an entire section of the Yajur devoted to optional animal sacrifices.

3   Indian philosopher Basant I. Lal, in an article in Tom Regan's book *Animal Sacrifices: Religious Perspectives on the Use of Animals in Science* states that the primary goal of every Hindu is to attain 'moksha', which involves performing religious rituals that will aid the achievement of that goal:

    '... the sacrifice of an animal is not really the killing of an animal. The animal to be sacrificed is not considered an animal; it is, instead, a symbol, a symbol of those powers for which the sacrificial ritual stands...... What is important for sacrificial ritual is not the object to be offered in sacrifice but following the elaborate rites and scrupulously observing the traditional rules.'

    So the fact that animals are sacrificed is not significant in Hindusim; the rituals performed when sacrificing are of greater significance in helping a Hindu to attain moksha.

Buddhism

Arguments against the use of animals

1   The interdependence of all living things is a fundamental belief of Buddhism – everything depends on everything else. Care for animals is therefore important and will enhance life. For example, during the festival of Wesak in countries such as Thailand, Buddhists buy caged birds and fish in order to set them free.

2   Buddha showed compassion for other animals in his own life e.g. he rescued an injured swan from his cousin. Buddhism, like Hinduism, teaches Ahimsa (non-violence).

3   At the time of the Buddha, eating meat was not forbidden, but members of the sangha were not allowed to kill animals for food or sport, or to farm them.

4   Some Buddhists are completely vegetarian, but generally Buddhists do not adopt a strict approach to vegetarianism, preferring to leave it to the individual's conscience, combined with the guidance found in Buddhist teachings such as the precepts e.g. 'I undertake to abstain from killing living beings'.

5   The doctrine of karma teaches that any wrong behaviour will have to be paid for in a future life, so cruel acts to animals should be avoided.

Arguments in favour of the use of animals

At the time of the Buddha, members of the sangha were allowed to eat meat that had been given to them by householders.

Task

Writing task	a) Explain the variety of attitudes within one major world religion to the issue of animal rights.
	b) 'Animals deserve the same moral status as other species such as humans'. Assess this view.

Glossary

ahimsa	The Hindu/Buddhist belief in non-violence
akra	The Muslim idea that we will be held accountable by God for our treatment of animals on the Day of Judgment
bloodsport	A sport that involves causing suffering to animals
culling	The killing of surplus animals as a means of population control
dominion	To have authority over something
factory farming	Mass production farming, based on the idea of maximising profit
halal	The permissible way for Muslims to kill an animal, by cutting its throat with a sharp blade so that it loses consciousness and dies as quickly and painlessly as possible
instrumental value	Only of value because it is useful to humans
intrinsic value	Worthy of value in itself, deserving a moral status
khalifa	A Muslim term meaning humans are guardians of God's creation
schechitah	The permissible way for Jews to kill an animal, by cutting its throat with a sharp blade so that it loses consciousness and dies as quickly and painlessly as possible
speciesism	The belief held by some that it is unjust to treat one species as being superior to another e.g. humans are superior to animals
stewardship	The mainly Christian belief that humans have a God given responsibility to manage or control the earth
tawhid	A Muslim term meaning all creatures are created by God
vegan	A person who does not eat, drink or use any animal products such as meat or leather
vegetarian	A person who does not eat meat, and sometimes other animal products, for moral, religious or health reasons

Religion and TV

Aim of the section

This section asks you to consider the ways in which religion is portrayed through the medium of television, specifically in soap operas, The Simpsons and religion-specific broadcasting.

This means that you will have to consider the following key matters:

▶ *the way that religious and moral themes are explored in soap operas;*

▶ *how The Simpsons portrays religious belief and practice;*

▶ *what the purpose of religion-specific broadcasting is;*

▶ *the effect the portrayal of religion within these areas is intended to have on the target audience;*

▶ *how effective each area is in portraying religious ideas.*

Religious Themes in Soap Operas

Aim

After studying this chapter you should be able to understand how religious and moral themes are explored within soap operas. You should also be able to evaluate how effective soap operas are in presenting beliefs and practices about religion.

The soap opera forms a major part of our entertainment industry. More people watch soap operas than any other type of entertainment and the viewing figures for some of our best-loved soaps eclipse weekly attendance figures at our places of worship. They are a tremendously significant (if not important!) part of daily life in the UK. Their influence on us as a society is also huge. The current storylines of any soap will often be found as central to a particular discussion in any group of people – from young children to the elderly – and everybody has a point of view. Perhaps it is this very inclusivity that makes soap opera so successful as an entertainment medium. They tend to reflect our own everyday experiences – from the repetition of daily rituals such as meal times and work, to the more extreme scandals involving sex, drugs and murder.

> **Seminar topic**
>
> **Soap operas can teach us nothing useful about religion or life.**

Television forms an important part of many people's lives.

Daniel Chandler gives a very useful introduction to the soap opera concept in his article *The TV Soap Opera Genre and its Viewers* (1994):

'*The soap opera genre originated in American radio serials of the 1930s, and owes the name to the sponsorship of some of these programmes by major soap powder companies. So, like many television genres (e.g. news and quiz shows), the soap opera is a genre originally drawn from radio rather than film.*

Television soap operas are long-running serials concerned with everyday life. The serial is not to be confused with the series, in which the main characters and format remain the same from programme to programme but each episode is a self-contained plot. In a serial at least one storyline is carried over from one episode to the next. A series is advertised as having a specific number of episodes, but serials are potentially endless.'

This definition shows how we can distinguish a soap opera from any other type of programme broadcast on our television networks. It is particularly useful in helping us avoid confusion between soap operas and other programmes that have established characters and are shown on a regular basis (e.g. a series such as *The Vicar of Dibley*).

Seminar topic

Should people be taught about religion through the medium of a soap opera?

Another useful view on soap operas – and why they hold such mass appeal, comes from an article by Merris Griffiths, *'Why are soap operas so popular?'* (1995):

'The ways in which soaps are fundamentally constructed also hold great appeal for the viewer. If one is to consider… the most significant British soaps….. it is plain that the focus is placed upon the inter-relationship of a group of characters in a typically working-class setting. Indeed, soap opera story lines are based largely on the problems encountered within personal relations and family life; the content is essentially humanised. A mundane quality is evoked, as the lifestyles of the characters on screen are not so vastly different from our own.

Seminar topic

If soap operas teach that there is no such thing as an 'objective truth', does that undermine the concept of religious authority?

Many claims have been made by the producers of these soaps, in that they are ultimately designed to represent the realities of working class life and confront social problems. Viewers do profess to gain pleasure from this social realism. Yet, at the same time, soaps do not claim to offer single solutions to the problems they portray, but explore all the relevant possibilities. There are no objective truths, no answers, no permanent securities, no uncompromised actions and no absolutes' … these features only serve to further emphasise that this genre really is reflective of a real life that holds few certainties for anyone.'

1. Livingstone, Sonia M. [1990]: Making Sense of Television. London: Pergamon Press

The role of religion in soaps is often understated – and that may well be deliberate. Programme makers are wary of offending faith communities, either by misrepresentation of a particular faith or by non-representation of it in comparison to others. However, there are universal themes which soap regularly use as the moral and spiritual backdrops to their characters' storylines. These include love; relationships; friendship; forgiveness; commitment; reconciliation; faithfulness; family; community; authority; responsibility; death. It is your ability to relate these sort of universal concepts to specific religious teaching that will help you in your studies.

Task

Writing task	In pairs or small groups, select five of the themes listed in the above paragraph.
	With reference to a soap opera that you have seen, record where those themes have been used and how they were portrayed in the soap (i.e. positively or negatively).

A contextual overview

The following material, based on the current (at the time of writing) highest ranking soap operas (in terms of viewing audience), is not intended to be exhaustive in its coverage of soap operas on British television. The examples are chosen to represent the main soap operas on television. Placing the soap in its intended context will allow a more accurate interpretation of the events shown within the programme itself:

1 Coronation Street

The longest running soap opera on British television, *Coronation Street*, has been broadcast since December 1960 and remains one of the highest ranking programmes on terrestrial television in the UK. It is set in the fictional Greater Manchester town of Weatherfield. The street itself is made up of terraced houses on one side – with its pub 'The Rover's Return' at one end of the street and a corner shop at the other. The pub is the centrepiece for much of the social interaction within the soap – a feature shared by both *Eastenders* with the 'Queen Vic' and *Emmerdale's* 'The Woolpack'.

The other side of the street comprises a garage, a factory, a few houses and two other shop units. These features give the show a variety of contexts for its residents (almost all of whom are in some way involved with the industrial, as well as residential, properties). In recent years the programme has extended its boundaries to include families who live in other adjoining streets.

The main focus of the show is the relationships between all of these individuals – within and outside their own families. The show also makes a conscious effort to include a variety of social classes and ages in its storylines.

Despite this, it has often been criticised for its under-representation of people of faith among its characters. There are sometimes allusions to people belonging to a particular faith community (e.g. Dev and Amber (Hindu)) but these are rarely made explicit or developed. Emily Bishop is often seen to be involved in the activities of her local church (Anglican), and even had a brief engagement in 1994 to the vicar, Bernard. Her character is well known for her moral principles and her sense of 'justice', but her actual religious character is otherwise unexplored within the soap.

Whilst religiousness itself is often largely ignored within the soap, the inclusion of rites of passage is, relatively speaking, standard fare. *Coronation Street* has had many weddings within its history and boasts proudly of the fact that, in 1981, more than 24 million people in the UK watched Ken Barlow and Deirdre Langton's wedding. This was more than the number of people who, two days later, watched the Prince of Wales marry Lady Diana Spencer.

What the soap lacks in portrayal of its characters' religious beliefs, it makes up for in the moral arena. Over its lengthy history, almost all characters have had to face moral dilemmas of some sort. As it is principally a drama rather a documentary, these moral dilemmas have often been quite extreme, including storylines about murder, domestic abuse, teenage pregnancies, adultery and trans-sexuality.

Many of these dilemmas are relatively common across soap operas; it is the way in which the characters respond that gives the soap its own sense of identity. In *Coronation Street*, the storylines often combine the very serious with the light-hearted and comic across its cast of characters – often to provide light relief from the difficult issues that it chooses to deal with. This allows the show to develop intense storylines without attracting the criticisms that soaps such as *Eastenders* often face of being 'too depressing'.

2 EastEnders

EastEnders was first broadcast by BBC1 in February 1985. The soap is set in the fictional London borough of Walford, and specifically in Albert Square – a Victorian square which comprises residences (houses and flats), a number of small businesses, a pub (the Queen Vic) and a street market. Much like *Coronation Street* it centres its storylines around the inhabitants of this specific setting, but has broadened out in recent years to try to give more of a sense of realism to the show. It is this realism that is arguably the defining characteristic of *EastEnders*.

The storylines of the show were originally based around a number of key families, although describing them as clans might be more accurate, due to the fact that these families have had large numbers of extended members joining the cast throughout its history. This has allowed the soap to explore in-depth the concept of the importance of family and the moral questions that arise from this.

Walford Market, Eastenders

From its very start *EastEnders* has included explicitly religious characters – most famously Dot Cotton (Christian) - although these portrayals have attracted strong criticism. The Sikh Messenger's editor, Dr. Indarijit Singh, accused the BBC of anti-religious bias, and specifically cited the soap:

'EastEnders' Dot Cotton is an example. She quotes endlessly from the Bible and it ridicules religion to some extent.'

Dr Chakravarthi Ram-Prasad of the Department of Religious Studies at the University of Lancaster has stated that:

'... soaps tend to use stereotypes - the Christians are mad fundamentalists, the Hindus are in arranged marriages.'

These criticisms were also echoed by the House of Lords' select committee (set up in 2005 to report on the future of the BBC), who saw in the show a number of examples of religion being deliberately undermined because of its stereotypical and inaccurate representations of people of faith communities. It was also admitted that the BBC as a corporation, had a very poor knowledge of religion and that ignorance permeated throughout its entire programming – often with a detrimental effect on its audience as a whole.

When it comes to moral issues, *EastEnders* has never been afraid to take on controversial storylines: rape, murder, child abuse, abortion, euthanasia, drugs, HIV, child abduction, amongst many others. The way in which *EastEnders* has dealt with many of these storylines has helped to raise public awareness of their existence. It is not uncommon for the soap to publish a helpline number relating to specific moral issues both before and after the programme is aired. (This practice has also been taken up by other soaps). Charities related to these issues often praise the soap for helping educate

Mary Whitehouse, who campaigned to uphold moral standards in television broadcasting

people about incredibly complex and difficult issues, recognising that for most people the information they learn about the issues comes from the television they watch. The other important factor to consider is that the soap is broadcast entirely 'pre-watershed' (i.e. before 9pm, which is considered to be the appropriate time after which young children will not have access to television) and yet it may deal with content that many believe belongs firmly after the watershed.

At a convention in 1987, where she was speaking about the decline in moral standards in television broadcasting, the late Mary Whitehouse (founder of the 'Clean Up TV Campaign' in the early 1960s) said:

'You may well wonder, and I would understand, why we keep such a close eye on BBC's 'EastEnders'. The reason is simple. This programme challenges many of the fundamental principles, which, on paper, govern the corporation's thinking about 'family viewing time'. The timing of this programme puts this whole concept at risk. And all in the name of the so-called 'battle for the ratings'. It has been scheduled opposite 'Coronation Street' which stood top of the polls for many years.

It is at our peril and at the children's peril too, that we allow 'EastEnders', with its verbal aggression and its atmosphere of physical violence, its homosexuals, its blackmailing pimp and its prostitute, its lies and deceits and its bad language, to go unchallenged. The fact that the programme is also strong on warmth, friendship and family loyalty is no justification for the emotional exploitation which characterises so many of its episodes.'

Seminar topic

Soap operas should not present material that might offend their audience.

There are a number of other well-known soaps on British television, each of which has a specific target audience; issues, both religious and moral, will be presented with that audience in mind. It is always useful to bear this context in mind when evaluating the way in which both religious and moral issues are dealt with by the programme.

Task

Research task	Choose any one soap and watch an episode. Each time a reference is made to either a religious or moral issue, make a written record.
	Select between one and three of those references and explain how each relates to the relevant religious/moral issue.

Identifying religious themes within a soap opera

The identification of themes that may be deemed 'religious' is a difficult task in terms of complete comprehensiveness; however, major themes such as beliefs, practices and ethical values are obvious starting points. You should note that reference to specifically religious contexts for the themes is essential, and it is not appropriate to use themes in a generic way. For example, forgiveness is both a religious and non-religious concept, and such a chosen theme will only be acceptable if reference to its religious context is explicitly stated.

So, an analysis might refer to a character from within the soap acting in a way that is actively seeking to avoid harming either another character or an animal. Whilst illustrating this with appropriate reference to the chosen soap, you could make clear that this is the Hindu concept of *ahimsa* being shown. In this way your analysis is clearly relating the actions from within the soap to a specific theme from religion.

Task

Presentation task	Choosing any one soap opera, prepare a PowerPoint presentation that illustrates how religious or moral themes are portrayed.
	(You should include either a video clip or excerpts from the script to support your presentation.)

Study of religious themes

In soaps, it should always be remembered that the prime objective of the programme is to tell a story. For this reason, characters, storylines and themes – religious or not – are only there to further the story. Religion is not usually explored for its own sake within a soap, but rather to add a dimension – or explain the motivation – of a specific person from within the story. It is very common to see caricatures of religious figures within soaps because of this e.g. Dot Cotton, in *EastEnders*, as a stereotypical church-going person, portrayed as a 'busybody' with a judgemental attitude which comes from her understanding of her own faith (needless to say this unfair image has attracted much criticism from Christian groups).

Other examples include the vicar, Ashley, in *Emmerdale*. When introduced as a character several years ago, his character was portrayed as weak and effeminate with a superficial faith, characterised by occasional quotes from biblical or church doctrine that were about 40 years out of date! Fortunately, and partly due to complaints from Christian groups, the character has developed into a more believable and sympathetic person, more accurately reflecting the typical rural Anglican vicar.

Portraying religious characters seems to be a difficult business for most soaps. Whilst caricatured Christians have appeared in most of the major soap operas, people from other faiths have fared even worse. Sensitivities to religious and cultural groups have seemingly compounded the problem. However, as mentioned earlier, there appear to be some positive, yet gradual, representations of people from other faith backgrounds starting to appear in soaps. Whilst this is an attempt to more accurately portray multi-cultural Britain, we need to remind ourselves, once again, that they are there to help drive the plot and further the storyline. As such, the representations of people of faith will often be skewed for a particular storytelling purpose. It is appropriate to remember how this is done and to explain whether or not such incidences might mislead the audience as to the actual belief/practice/teaching of the religion.

Tasks

Research task	As a class, divide up the responsibility to watch a number of different soaps. List any characters that are shown to be religious. Collate your findings as a class — listing the positive and negative ways that the characters' religious behaviour is portrayed.

Writing task	a. Explain how moral issues are dealt with by soap operas.
	b. 'Soap operas oversimplify complex moral problems.'
	Assess this view.

Glossary

adult content	Content which may include graphic violence; nudity, explicit sex; drug use; strong language
ahimsa	The Hindu concept of non-harm or non-violence
objective truth	A truth that is true in any circumstances, regardless of people's feelings or situations
soap opera	A long-running serial concerned with everyday life
stereotype	Fixed, commonly held notion or image of a person or group, based on an oversimplification of some observed or imagined trait of behaviour or appearance
watershed	A time in television schedules, commonly seen as 9.00pm, after which it is permissible to show programmes that contain adult content

Religious beliefs and practices in *The Simpsons*

Aim

After studying this chapter you should understand how religious belief and practice is examined through episodes of The Simpsons. You should also be able to produce your own analysis of the portrayal of religious belief and practice within the show.

Religion and The Simpsons: an overview

"Are you there, God? It's me, Bart Simpson."

In many ways this quote, taken from the *Bart Sells His Soul* episode, sums up the relationship between this long-running animated sitcom (at the time of writing, in its nineteenth season) and religion. Its characters, much like a mirror to western society, range from those who are committed believers (e.g. Marge, Ned Flanders, Apu) to those who appear to use religion as a crutch to get them through the more difficult times in their lives (e.g. Homer, Bart, Krusty) but otherwise have little interest in following a religious lifestyle. As observers of the show have noted, religion itself has never been mocked outright by the show:

'The show always is kind to people of true faith, but people who build their religion on words and not feelings are treated less kindly.' Jeff Shalda, Religion in the Simpsons, 2000

When a show is as satirical as *The Simpsons*, it is sometimes difficult to overcome the sense that everything in it is portrayed in a mocking manner. The use of cartoon animation invites the viewer to see the content of the show in a child-like way, but this is deceptive: it is just part of the brilliance of Groening's creativity that his material is not only popular entertainment, but also relevant, incisive and, most important, a commentary on contemporary society. The use of religion within the show is part of this, but the creators and writers are even handed in their treatment of religion – as they try to be with all of the facets of human (and occasionally, alien) life that they deal with. The writers of the show come from a variety of faith standpoints, ranging from atheist to agnostic to theist, as well as being representative, in background at least, of a variety of mainly Christian and Jewish traditions. Faith communities are also, occasionally, consulted so that details of religious belief and practice are accurately portrayed within the show.

Mark Pinsky's seminal *The Gospel according to The Simpsons* (2nd edition, 2007) states:

'Rabbi Lavi Meier and Rabbi Harold Schulweis, a leading thinker of Conservative Judaism in America, served as "special technical consultants"….the two rabbis' expertise and guidance is apparent throughout the show.'

'Schulweis . . . said he was surprised to find how genuine it [the Like Father, Like Clown episode] was. "I thought it had a Jewish resonance to it. It was profound. I was impressed by the underlying moral seriousness."'

It is not only leading thinkers of the Jewish community who have noted this *'underlying moral seriousness'*. Within the Anglican Communion, the Archbishop of Canterbury, Dr Rowan Williams, has said of the show:

'The Simpsons is one of the most subtle pieces of propaganda around in the cause of sense, humility and virtue'.

Pinsky gives a long list of such quotations from a variety of well respected religious sources, all supporting what is being done with the show, as a vehicle for promoting values that cohere with religious teaching. Admittedly, the initial reaction in America, particularly amongst conservative groups, was less than favourable to the antics of the show but Davis Landry, the Roman Catholic theologian and biblical scholar, is quoted as saying:

'This is not the be-all and end-all of theology on TV, but the most consistent and intelligent treatment of religion on TV is on The Simpsons.'

As the series continues to grow, so too do the episodes that include religious and moral teaching. When asked whether they believed the show was trying to teach religious values, the actors who portray the characters were adamant that it was not. This view is upheld by some religious groups in America who regard the show with mistrust and suspicion, seeing it as a veiled attack on their beliefs and practices. It would appear, however, that the evidence for these claims would not be out of place in John Wisdom's famous parable about the garden – where two men cannot agree on whether the evidence they have in front of them suggests that there is a gardener or that there is no gardener.

Task

Research task	Find a copy of John Wisdom's *Parable of the Gardener*. What point do you think the author of the parable is trying to make?

When looking at the show, members of the atheist tradition have accused it of being 'more like a Sunday school lesson than a sitcom.' (Pinsky) Acknowledging the satire of *The Simpsons*, some have claimed that the series is actually the most religious, non-evangelical, show on television. 'While other programs avoid the issue of religion, *The Simpsons* takes religion's place in society seriously enough to do it the honour of making fun of it.' (John Sohn, *Simpson Ethics*)

Tasks

Writing task	Using an episode of *The Simpsons*, list as many religious references as you can find. For five of these references, explain carefully how they relate to religious belief and practice. It may be appropriate to make reference to sources of religious authority to do this (e.g. Scripture, Traditions, etc.) *(Recommended episodes: Homer the Heretic; Lisa the Sceptic; Like Father, Like Clown; In Marge We Trust).*
Research task	1 As a class, using an approved database source such as the episode guide from **www.thesimpsons.com** draw up a list of episodes that are specifically related to religion. A minimum of ten episodes is suggested, but if your teaching group exceeds this number you may wish to draw up a list that matches the number of students in the class. 2 Each student should watch a different episode. Record in writing how religion is portrayed within your episode and prepare a presentation on your findings for the class.

Meeting the Family: an overview of *The Simpsons*

Whilst the show's animated cast now numbers in the hundreds, the family always represents the core of any episode. Each member has come to take on an almost archetypal status within the popular imagination of many people today. Contained within each is a set of characteristics which can be easily identified, as well as related to, by the audience.

The following is the character summary given by Jeff Shalda:

Marge, the 34-year-old mother of the family, is the glue that holds the family together. Her sense of morality, and selfless commitment to her family is the only thing that keeps 'The Simpsons' from falling apart. This directly affects her views on religion. She is a devout Christian, who looks to God and religion to give her the strength necessary to keep her family going. Because of this, her prayers are often bargains with God, such as when the town is facing a nuclear meltdown Marge prays, "Dear Lord, if you spare this town from becoming a smoking hole in the ground, I'll try to be a better Christian, I don't know what I can do . . . Mmm . . . oh, the next time there's a canned food drive, I'll give the poor something they'll actually like instead of old lima beans and pumpkin mix" ('Homer Defined'). She views the church as the only place to curb Homer and Bart's appetites, if only for an hour a week.

Marge Simpson

Lisa is, without a doubt, the smartest eight-year-old in Springfield. She is light years ahead of anyone else in her family intellectually, and this shows on many levels. Her intelligence causes her to view religion as a matter of a set of morals and tradition rather than of pure faith. She views things as causes and effects. For example, if she watches stolen cable, she will go to hell, therefore she should not watch it ('Lisa vs. Homer' and 'The 8th Commandment'). Or, when she cheats on a test she feels she must confess because her morals dictate that she should, even though if she does the school will lose funding ('Lisa Gets an A'). Although she is rather incapable of taking leaps of faith, her strong sense of morality leads her to live a good life anyway, and to try her best to influence other family members to do so. (She later chooses Buddhism as an appropriate expression for her spiritual nature.)

Lisa Simpson

Bart Simpson

Bart is the ten-year-old anarchist whose goal in life seems to be to rebel against any form of authority he can find. These include his parents, his teachers, the town, and the ultimate authority, God. However, like most rebellious kids, Bart ultimately seeks the control of the very things he rebels against. That is why most of his "pranks are either thwarted or turn to ultimate good" (Bowler, par. 27). Bart is the prodigal son of the family, and through him, the others' good nature is allowed to shine. For example, when Bart ruins Christmas for the family, and then lies about it, they end up losing everything to the angry townsfolk. However, from this they learn to appreciate each other and realize that Christmas is not about material possessions ('Miracle on Evergreen Terrace').

Homer is the 36 year-old patriarch of the Simpson family. He is the dimwitted nucleus of the family, but he depends on the others far more than they depend on him. His views on religion are best described as confused. He constantly misreads the Bible, such as when he tells Lisa,

Homer Simpson

"your mother has this crazy idea that gambling is wrong, even though they say it's okay in the Bible". When Lisa asks where, Homer replies, "somewhere in the back" ('Springfield'). He also mistakes God for a waffle stuck to the ceiling ('Homer Loves Flanders'), and believes that Hercules and the Lion is a Bible story ('Blood Feud'). This confusion leads Homer to constantly fall into sin, however: "Catholics would say his sins are venial, rather than mortal. He willingly does wrong, but never rejects God or the idea of divine justice. He's simply weak" (Kisken, par. 31). And although he is, for the most part, a sinner, his dedication to his family is why he ultimately ends up choosing good over evil.

Task

Writing task	Choose two other characters from *The Simpsons* and write a pen portrait of each one, concentrating on their attitude towards religion

Finding religion in *The Simpsons*: a practical guide

The key to any successful examination answer on this topic is to be able to analyse what *The Simpsons* says about religion as well as being able to comment on how they say it. This is possible as long as we have relevant information to hand on:

a. Religious belief and practice;

b. The specific context within *The Simpsons*.

Currently there is no better overview guide to the way in which *The Simpsons* deals with religion than Mark Pinsky's *Gospel according to the Simpsons* (reprinted in 2007 with the subtitle: *'bigger and possibly even better edition'*). From the way in which God is presented, to religious beliefs and practices – as well as denominational and different faith representations – the book deals in detail with these themes, usually by presenting the reader with an in-depth synopsis of a specific episode that illustrates the theme being discussed. It is recommended that you familiarise yourself with this text.

Remember, when watching a particular episode, it may be that there is no overtly religious theme being explored. (Remember! This is an animated comedy that satirises life, not a theological text).

For example, in one episode, where the town is divided into districts according to its telephone area dialling codes (*A Tale of Two Springfields*), a remark is made by Carl to Lenny about the significance of the numbers being used as the area codes (these being 636 and 939):

"I'm not sure which one's better. The '6' is closer to the '3', so you got convenience there, but the '9' has less to do with Satan, which is a plus in this religious world of ours."

This is the only time that religion explicitly features in the episode but it is significant that without an understanding of Judeo-Christian numerology, where 7 is regarded as the perfect number and 6 as imperfect, this comment would make little sense. In addition, Carl's statement that the world is 'religious' is interesting for two reasons:

first, Carl is never presented as a particularly religious individual – such a line might be more expected from Ned Flanders. Second, the show's writers are putting words into the mouth of one of the more 'normal' characters from within the show, perhaps suggesting that the 'ordinary person' has not disposed of the idea of religion in their own minds, despite evidence which suggests that organised religion is in a state of decline within the western world.

Task

Writing task	
	1 Using the above example as a guide, identify any one instance in an episode of *The Simpsons* where religion is mentioned.
	2 Generate as many ideas as possible within the group, linking the religious context of the show with the relevant external religious contexts (e.g. beliefs, practices, etc.)
	3 Using the ideas that you have generated, write one or two paragraphs that explain how the show's religious reference relates to real world religious contexts.

The following sections are examples of how certain religions elements are portrayed within the show.

Scriptures

Like many of the targets for satire within the show, scripture (which is almost always the Bible) is not, in itself, mocked or treated in an irreverent way. However, the way in which others make use of scripture is frequently used to make a point about ignorance, hypocrisy or other negative behaviour.

Reverend Lovejoy is fond of using scripture to reinforce his point – whether it be within a sermon or in conversation with others. However, the way in which he makes use of the Bible is illuminating in itself. The harshness of certain parts of the Old Testament are often chosen by Lovejoy as his themes when preaching. The New Testament values of love, peace and reconciliation are rarely used by him. By doing this the show's creators would be seem to be exaggerating the point that some preachers prefer the 'hell and damnation' version of religion, for a variety of different reasons (e.g. it gives them power over the congregation; promotes fear of punishment and therefore of authority figures in religion; leads to increased subservience within the congregation etc.).

Lovejoy's application of the Bible is also inconsistent, ranging from quoting accurate references to Homer in *Homer the Heretic*, to the deliberate invention of verses to suit his own purposes (as was the case in the *Whacking Day* episode). By doing these things, Lovejoy undermines his own position as someone who is entrusted with safeguarding the authority of the scriptures – possibly for comedic effect within the show but possibly also so that the show's writers can make a social comment which they think is important.

Worship

The main focus for worship within the show is at the local Springfield Community Church (sometimes referred to as the First Church of Springfield), where the Reverend Lovejoy is minister in charge. Pinsky describes him as follows:

Rev. Lovejoy, preaching

'. . . the minister is hypocritical and occasionally venal, but he is not evil or immoral, merely human . . . He once had idealistic dreams for the ministry until, after decades in the pulpit, he came down with a classic case of preacher burnout. His sermons are boring, and he knows it. For the most part, the pastor provides an example of what a minister should not be.'

Other places of worship that are mentioned, and occasionally shown, are the Episcopalian Church (often referred to in terms of envy by Lovejoy and his supporters); The Catholic Church; and the local Synagogue.

Ironically enough, the congregation of Lovejoy's church seems to encompass the whole range of the Springfield community (a point made in *The Simpsons Movie*), although this may be more for the sake of the storyline than for any other reason. The actual worship that goes on within these services often seems to be non-participatory – that is, it seems that it does not matter whether the congregation is present or not. Notable exceptions to this are when something unusual happens – such as Lovejoy entertaining his congregation with the account of how he rescued Flanders from the baboons at the local zoo (*In Marge we Trust*); the congregation's enthusiastic participation in singing Bart's 'hymn' version of Iron Butterfly's *In A-Gadda-Da-Vida* rock masterpiece (re-entitled by Bart as *In the Garden of Eden*) (*Bart Sells His Soul*); and Grampa Simpson's religious experience in *The Simpson's Movie*, a take on the 'Toronto blessing', when an individual (or group) in the congregation is 'slain in the spirit' and behaves as if in receipt of some ecstatic gifts.

Other religious traditions

Springfield occasionally showcases other religious traditions and their forms of worship within certain episodes. In the 2005 episode *The Father, The Son and The Holy guest Star*, the **Roman Catholic** Church is given a satirical treatment – largely at the expense of stereotypes about Irish Catholicism and theology laced with guilt.

The **Jewish** tradition is represented, in the main, by Krusty the clown and his previously estranged father, Rabbi Hyman Krustofski. It would appear from the Rabbi's dress that he is a member of the Hasidim. As a strictly orthodox Jew the Rabbi does not endorse his son's chosen profession, seeing it as 'shameful'. In one of the most prominently Jewish themed episodes so far, *Like Father, Like Clown*, Jewish prayers, practices, rituals and philosophies abound.

Brian Rosman, a health policy researcher quoted by Pinsky, asserts:

"The Simpsons demonstrates a more intuitive understanding of American Jewish history, Jewish religion and culture, and Judaism's place among all the other varieties of belief and identity in America."

The **Buddhist** tradition has become represented in recent years by the character of Lisa Simpson. Ever mindful of the hypocrisies and perceived shortcomings of her own family's religious traditions, Lisa (portrayed as a sceptic) finally rejects the Christian tradition after the Community Church sells out to Mr Burns in order to rebuild, after an accident caused by Homer and Bart inadvertently destroys it. This rejection leads Lisa on a journey through a myriad of places of worship until she comes across a Buddhist Temple.

Class discussion

Using the stimulus 'Worship in Springfield is worthless, yet everybody does it', divide the class into two.

One group should take the argument that worship is for the good of the community and collect evidence from the show to support this.

The other group should take the opposing view, also collecting evidence to support their case.

At the end of the debate the class should vote on which side is able to make a more convincing case.

*Lisa Simpson,
meditating with
Richard Gere*

The inclusion of Richard Gere in this episode as one of America's most well-known Buddhists (he is a devout follower of Tibetan Buddhism) lends an authenticity to the Buddhist teachings which follow. Lisa embraces the philosophies of the pursuit of enlightenment, which can occur without the need for many of the perceived trappings of her former religious tradition. The concepts of meditation, the philosophies of impermanence, the four noble truths and the noble eightfold path, are all promoted within this episode.

Apu Nahasapeemapetilon is the show's main **Hindu** character. Although other Hindu characters have appeared, (including a priest and Apu's own family), it is usually through Apu that the religion is represented. His character is undeniably stereotypical but this may be due to the fact that for the show's American audience, Hinduism is one of the less well-known religious traditions of the world. His own devotion is to Ganesha of whom he keeps a murti in his convenience store, although he does make reference to other deities, particularly Shiva and Vishnu.

Episodes which deal with Apu's impending arranged marriage, Lisa becoming a vegetarian, his expressions of love for his wife during the Valentine's Day episode, and his trip back to India to renew his licence as a convenience store clerk (a stereotype within itself), all give an opportunity for the show to look at several key Hindu concepts, including those of vegetarianism; meditation; reincarnation; pluralism; and cultural assimilation.

Apu and family

Task

Writing task	'Religious traditions, other than Christianity, are always stereotyped in The Simpsons.' Assess this view.

Conclusion

The popularity of the The Simpsons ensures that it will have been watched by millions of people across the world. Its impact upon society is worthy of comment – which is why so many academic studies are now being devoted to it. Its portrayal of the human condition, whether deliberate or not, is part of the reason for its success. Within this portrayal, religious belief and practice are given the place they deserve, unlike any other show on television.

In his article *God and The Simpsons*, Gerry Bowler has this to say of the show's functionality:

Homer and Bart with the Flanders clan

'There is one more thing that 'The Simpsons' can tell us. If, as I suggest, it is among the most religious programmes on television it can only mean that religion is very badly served on that

medium . . . where else is religion to be found on television? Where do the denizens of 'Friends' go to church? What do we know about the spiritual life of 'Roseanne' or 'Frasier'? Are the doctors on 'ER' or 'Chicago Hope' ever moved to pray or consider God? Religion's invisibility in prime-time programming speaks volumes about how the entertainment industry views its place on the scale of human activity and until that changes we may have to make do with Ned Flanders as our televised spiritual mentor.

Seminar topic

Does The Simpsons have anything useful to teach us about the way people hold and practise religious beliefs?

The Simpsons is not afraid to hold up a mirror to society and, through its characters, show us ourselves. It is this function that underpins its importance. Bart's prayer (*Are you there God?*) is answered time and time again by the events and people around him. The Simpsons' relationship with religion looks like one that, much like the show itself, will continue to grow.

Glossary

cultural assimilation	When an individual or group becomes part of another culture and adopts it, whilst still retaining their own culture
heretic	A person who holds a 'false belief' or a set of beliefs that are contrary to the accepted orthodoxy of a particular religion or belief system
pluralism	The belief that there are many different paths to God, all equally valid
sceptic	A person who doubts belief in the religious or supernatural

Religion-specific Broadcasting

Aim

After studying this chapter you should be able to understand the purpose of religion-specific broadcasting and why we have it. You should also be able to evaluate how effective religion-specific broadcasting is in presenting beliefs and practices about religion.

Overview

Billy Graham, one of the best-known Christian evangelists of the latter part of the 20th Century, once stated that:

"Television is the most powerful communication ever devised by man."

Millions of people across the world watch television. For some, particularly those restricted within their homes, perhaps due to infirmity or disability, it is their sole link to the outside world. With the advent of the digital age, transmissions have risen so that there are literally thousands of broadcasting networks operating internationally.

Billy Graham

Even within the UK's terrestrial network, there are five channels available and with the introduction of satellite and cable television into British homes over the past 20 years, people now have access to hundreds of channels on a daily basis.

Indeed, with the process of all televisions moving to a digital, rather than analogue, signal (known as the 'Digital switchover'), far more channels are now freely available to people than before.

Television plays an important part in many people's lives.

'In 2009, Wales will begin the switchover to digital TV – becoming one of the first parts of the country to do so. The process will be completed in Wales by early 2010.'
(source: www.digitaluk.co.uk)

Many of these channels are 'specialist' channels, which deal with a narrow focus of programming: these include news, documentary, music, sport and religion. We are primarily interested in religion within this chapter, but it is not just within specialised channels that we find religious programming. All five of the British terrestrial channels are obliged, by the television agency Ofcom, to provide a minimum content of religion-specific broadcasts.

Task

Research task	1 Using the Internet, make a list of at least fifteen religiously themed programmes that have appeared on terrestrial television within the last ten years.
	2 Choose any three from the list and write a brief synopsis of what the programme was about, what its target audience was and how successful it was, in terms of viewing audience figures.

Many of these are familiar to us, such as *Songs of Praise* and *The Heaven and Earth Show*, but the extent of religious programming goes beyond these. In recent times there has been a conscious effort to promote wider understanding by making programmes which reflect an increasingly multi-faith Britain. In a survey published in May 2005, television industry professionals reported that they still believed that this had some way to go. Many people did recognise that religious programming devoted to specific periods within the religious calendar (i.e. festivals) were being increasingly well served and pointed to examples which reflected not only Christmas and Easter, but also Divali and Ramadan.

Task

Research task	Using the Internet, research the role of Ofcom and find out what responsibilities it has in relation to television broadcasting and religious programming in particular.

Why is it important for television programming to be regulated?

Religious programming has long been a feature of radio broadcasting. The *Thought for the Day* (Radio 4) and *Pause for Thought* (Radio 2) programme slots are well received and attract a large number of listeners. Part of the success of these programmes is that they are consciously multi-faith. This manner of programming is one which certain television programmes such as *The Heaven and Earth Show* have been trying to emulate.

When it comes to control over religious programming, there are strict guidelines which need to be followed. The following extract is from Section 4 of the Broadcasting Code which is supplied and monitored by Ofcom:

Principles

1 To ensure that broadcasters exercise the proper degree of responsibility with respect to the content of programmes which are religious programmes.

2 To ensure that religious programmes do not involve any improper exploitation of any susceptibilities of the audience for such a programme.

3 To ensure that religious programmes do not involve any abusive treatment of the religious views and beliefs of those belonging to a particular religion or religious denomination.

Rules

4.1 Broadcasters must exercise the proper degree of responsibility with respect to the content of programmes which are religious programmes.

Meaning of a "religious programme":

A religious programme is a programme which deals with matters of religion as the central subject, or as a significant part, of the programme.

4.2 The religious views and beliefs of those belonging to a particular religion or religious denomination must not be subject to abusive treatment.

4.3 Where a religion or religious denomination is the subject, or one of the subjects, of a religious programme, then the identity of the religion and/or denomination must be clear to the audience.

4.4 Religious programmes must not seek to promote religious views or beliefs by stealth.

4.5 Religious programmes on television services must not seek recruits. This does not apply to specialist religious television services. Religious programmes on radio services may seek recruits.

Meaning of "seek recruits":

Seek recruits means directly appealing to audience members to join a religion or religious denomination.

4.6 Religious programmes must not improperly exploit any susceptibilities of the audience.

4.7 Religious programmes that contain claims that a living person (or group) has special powers or abilities must treat such claims with due objectivity and must not broadcast such claims when significant numbers of children may be expected to be watching (in the case of television), or when children are particularly likely to be listening (in the case of radio).

These guidelines are designed to promote religious programming within a multicultural context. They are further explained in accompanying non-statutory guidance, which looks at certain aspects of the code and gives more detail to help clarify certain significant aspects.

For reflection

1 Think about the programmes that you watch on television.

2 How much influence do they have on how you choose to live your life?

3 Do you think television programming should have a role in promoting religious ideas?

Examples of religion-specific broadcasting

Songs of Praise

First aired in 1961, *Songs of Praise* has become, arguably, the best-known example of religion-specific broadcasting on television. It is, at the time of writing, the only religion specific programme to be shown at a peak viewing time within Europe on a non-subscription channel. It attracts an average of 4 million viewers each week, although this figure does fluctuate at certain times of the year. This is true of seasonal occasions, such as Christmas (e.g. *Carols from Kings*) and Easter, as well as at times when there is a focal point – usually bereavement – for the nation as a whole (e.g. the deaths of Winston Churchill and Princess Diana). At times such as these the viewing figures can rise to nearly 12 million.

Aled Jones, presenter, Songs of Praise

Task

Research task	Using the website: **www.bbc.co.uk/religion**, find out about the history of the show *Songs of Praise*, and produce a written report which includes details of how it has developed as an example of religion-specific broadcasting.

The Heaven and Earth Show

For nine years this programme was broadcast on Sunday mornings by BBC1. It was notable for its magazine format and multi-belief system approach. Representatives from faith communities, as well as those who were agnostic or atheist, were often included within the studio debates that took place. Guests from across the belief spectrum were common place, which was something of a departure from previously broadcast religious programmes on the British television network, at least.

The Heaven and Earth Show

International celebrities were also included on the show to discuss matters relating to their views on religion or ethics – Dolly Parton, Pierce Brosnan, John Barrowman and Lionel Richie all made appearances. It also had a live, interactive format and initially viewers were able to phone into the show; then, in later years, phone texts and e-mails were also included.

The Heaven and Earth Show was replaced in the autumn of 2007 by *The Big Questions*, which endeavoured to adopt a more panel based approach to religious and ethical dilemmas and ultimate questions – a similar format to the political discussion programme *Question Time*. Celebrity guests have again been a feature of this show – a deliberate device of the programme makers to encourage the viewing audience to identify common perspectives on belief with celebrities who would not normally seem to have any particular religious or ethical viewpoint (due to the context of their chosen world of entertainment).

Seminar topic

Do celebrities help people to relate to religious and ethical perspectives more easily?

Highway

Over a ten-year period, from 1983 to 1993, this was ITV's answer to the BBC's *Songs of Praise*. The format of the show involved hymns being sung by different groups and soloists. Interviews with people of faith were also a common feature of the show. During its history the show travelled across Britain, to meet different people in different communities, where they would usually be interviewed by the show's presenter, the late Sir Harry Secombe. *Highway* was initially scheduled for an early Sunday evening broadcast but towards the end of its run it moved to a Sunday afternoon slot.

Swansea born Harry Secombe – one of the 20th century's most popular presenters of religion-specific broadcasting

Documentaries

In order to attract a wider audience to religion-specific type broadcasting, a number of programme makers have tried a different approach. Much of this has been encapsulated within a documentary style approach, but these in themselves have ranged from straightforward 'fact-reporting' to 'fly-on-the-wall'. Topics such as conversion and marriage in Judaism; the 'Toronto Blessing'; the birth and death of Jesus of Nazareth; the Mormons; gay Christians in 21st Century Wales, etc. have all been addressed within these formats. Programmes such as *Everyman, Despatches* and *Witness* have all presented important religious and moral themed programmes. Audience figures for each of these programmes also suggest that there is interest from the wider television viewing public. Such programmes, therefore, will continue to be made to help meet this clear demand.

It is also important to realise that dedicated documentary channels such as *The History Channel, Discovery* and *National Geographic*, regularly (and increasingly) broadcast religion specific documentaries. Other popular 'reality' religious programmes have also attracted a wide audience, including *The Monastery; An Island Parish;* and *Extreme Pilgrim*.

Seminar topic

What do you think were the main purposes of the shows mentioned above?

Do you think that they were successful in what they set out to do?

Seminar topic

How effective are religious 'reality' programmes (e.g. An Island Parish, The Monastery, etc.) in promoting their specific religious beliefs, values, practices and traditions to a television audience?

Outside of terrestrial 'free-to-air' television channels, the introduction of satellite/digital television has revolutionised the content available to the viewing public of the 21st Century. For every interest there is a wealth of channels, and religion is no exception to this rule. Current British digital channel access has a number of religion-specific channels, of which Christian channels currently take up the largest percentage. This is also mirrored in the increasing provision of religion-specific dedicated radio channels.

The website **www.ChristianSat.org.uk** maintains a list of Christian channels currently available within the UK (seventeen, at the time of writing). These channels vary in terms of their denominational source, as well as country of origin, although the evangelical aspect of Christianity is particularly well represented.

Task

Research task	Using the 'ChristianSat' web address (listed above), write down details relating to the target audience of five of these channels. Find out the content of their peak viewing time schedules and record these findings. Are there similarities between them or are they very different? Explain your findings in your teaching group.

Other religious traditions are represented in a similarly growing number of dedicated religion-specific channels. (e.g. mta – Muslim TV; channel Punjab; Islam channel; Zee TV, etc.) One of the interesting features for many of these channels is that the religion is very closely tied into the language of that community and therefore, by its nature, tends to be exclusive to that particular faith community.

Some of the other religious channels available on British digital television

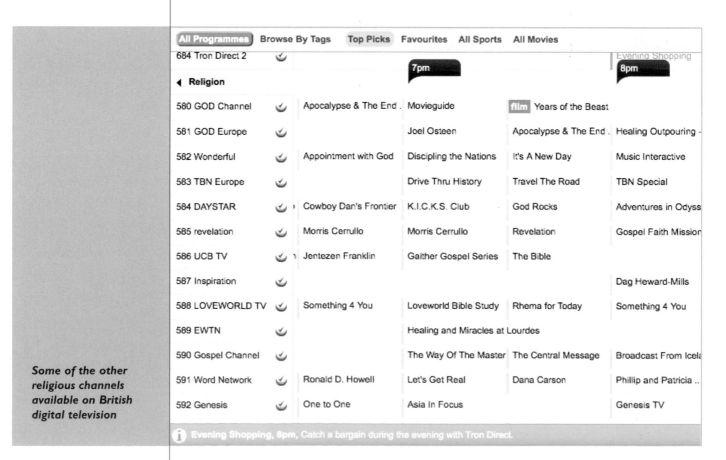

This is especially true for Hindu, Muslim and Sikh communities, although there are magazine programmes available on all these networks that tend to reflect the main language of the country of origin. English subtitles are also a common feature on many of these channels, reflecting the fact that for a significant proportion of the channels' audience, English is the only language to which they have fluent access. This is a very common feature for younger members of certain faith communities.

TV representations of religion: intense debate or traditional ritual?

Task

Writing task	'Religious channels should be as inclusive as possible, in order to attract the widest possible audience.' Discuss this point of view.

A possible future for religion-specific broadcasting in the UK

Whilst *Songs of Praise* continues to run, other religion-specific programmes do not enjoy the same longevity. Is this because the television viewing public do not want religion as a feature of their television diet? This question has been carefully researched and the answer has been resoundingly in favour of religious content. The aspect that appears to have changed within the last ten years is how television executives have defined religion-specific broadcasting.

Previously, the definition has been rather narrow. Programming has tended to be little more than a mirror of particular services and events, interviewing people and presenting the religion at face value. In recent years, largely due to increased public pressure, a wider definition of religion-specific broadcasting has been adopted, to include, amongst other things, a more informative and investigative approach towards religion.

The Ofcom report of May 2005 also noted that there were three main types of religious programming being asked for by the viewing public. These are as follows:

1   *Worship-style programming*

    Along the lines of the long-running *Songs of Praise*, respondents to Ofcom's survey felt that it was appropriate to have a programme which reflected a 'service of worship'. This did not necessarily have to be from one tradition only, but could derive from any of the religious traditions present within the UK today. It was also felt appropriate to have people of faith interviewed, to show how their 'faith affected their lives, culture and life in the widest sense'.

2   *Informative programming*

    Whether from a faith background or not, all respondents to the Ofcom survey were keen to see an increase in programmes that informed about religious issues, beliefs and practices in the modern world. Concern was expressed that much of the information given to people in the current mass media tended to concentrate on extremists or stereotypes and it was felt that a more objective view towards these religious traditions could help towards a wider understanding of different beliefs and practices, thereby promoting a greater degree of tolerance towards these traditions.

    Documentaries were seen as a particularly good way of transmitting information about aspects of people's lives that 'are shared across the faiths but which are played out differently e.g. weddings, funerals.' Global events, such as the events of September 11th 2001, were cited as triggers for increased access to such informative programming. The exploration of world history, as seen through the eyes of a particular faith tradition, was also something that respondents wanted to see in television programming. Programmes such as *Witness* and *Everyman* were seen as particularly good at meeting these demands.

3   *Inclusion into mainstream programming*

    As mentioned in the previous two chapters, religion does play a role in programmes that are not specifically dedicated to it. However, the survey showed that people felt that the current depiction of religious traditions within mainstream programming was too superficial, stereotyped and, at worst, unhelpful. It was felt that a real reflection 'of how many people have a faith, and how much faith plays a part in their lives and everyday decision-making' was needed within such programmes, so that the viewing audience received a more accurate depiction of British life and how people of faith responded to it. The use of soaps, in particular, was highlighted as an excellent way of transmitting information about 'moral messages', particularly for the younger section of the viewing public. The effectiveness of television as a communication medium was cited as one of the main reasons that it needed to take its role in presenting moral and religious ideas more accurately than it was felt it did at present.

    This thirst for religious programming seems to demonstrate that whilst attendance at traditional places of worship may be declining in the UK, interest in religious and moral matters is not. (This issue is explored in more depth in Section 3 of this book.) The challenge to the television networks is how to respond to this obvious interest from the viewing public.

Why do you think it is important that children are taught about different religions from a young age?

Task

Research task	Making use of a television guide, try to find at least three examples of religion-specific broadcasting – across all networks – that fit into the three categories mentioned above. Give a brief explanation as to why each programme belongs to its category.

Religion-specific programming in non-religion-specific broadcasts

Over recent years, programmers have been increasingly creative in the way in which they have presented religion to the viewing public. In the young children's television programmes *The Fimbles, The Tweenies* and *Teletubbies*, faith communities have been visited, showcased and explained to the audience in terms of festivals and ritual practices – using the vivid images often associated with these events to promote understanding of different cultures and belief systems.

These opportunities have been widely welcomed by the leaders of faith communities who sit on advisory panels to the television networks, as being positive examples of religion on television.

Other examples include incidental appearances of religious individuals and communities within regular programming such as soaps and series, documentaries (e.g. those shown on *The History Channel* and *National Geographic*), even comedies. *The Vicar of Dibley* took a light-hearted look at an issue which for many Anglicans was very difficult when it was first aired – that of female ordination to the priesthood. *Goodness Gracious Me* and

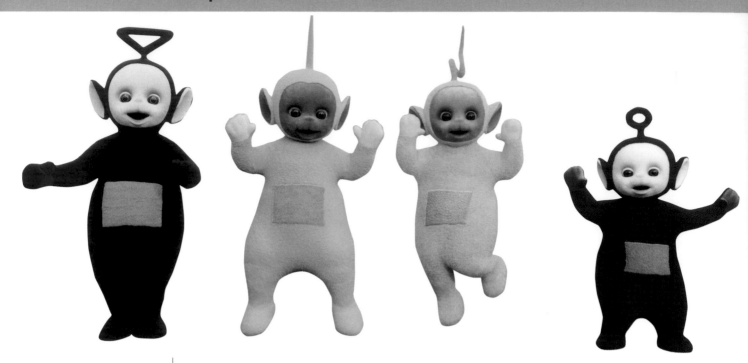

The Kumars at No 42 have both addressed issues that relate to the Asian faith communities (typically Hinduism, Islam and Sikhism) in Britain, again with the use of gentle, almost self-deprecating humour. In 2007 a Canadian network premiered the comedy *Little Mosque on the Prairie* (a deliberate play on the title of the internationally famous *Little House on the Prairie* television series that ran from 1974-1983).

Little Mosque on the Prairie tells the story of a small community of Muslims living in a small prairie town in Canada and the trials they face there – both within their own community and in the wider community of the town where they live. Again, using a mixture of gentle comedy and self-deprecating humour, the show has looked at some of the issues which have caused huge problems for the Muslim community in the West and presented them in such a way as to dispel many of the myths that have caused so much social and political tension since the events of September 11th 2001.

Comedy is a useful way of explaining religion to people in a non-threatening way.

Task

Writing task	
	a. Describe the main features of religion specific broadcasting.
	b. 'Religion-specific broadcasting is essential in today's world'. Assess this view.

Glossary

free-to-air	Description of any television channel that does not require its viewers to pay to watch its programmes.
Ofcom	The regulatory body that oversees all television broadcasting.
self-deprecating	Conscious of your own shortcomings
terrestrial	Networks in the UK confined to BBC1, BBC2, ITV1, C4 and C5

Section 3

Aim of the section

This section asks you to consider the diversity of ideas about the influence of religion in society, the phenomenon of religious fundamentalism and the emergence of new religious movements.

This means you will have to consider the following key matters:

- ▶ *the definition of religion;*

- ▶ *the concept of secularisation and its six main elements;*

- ▶ *the reasons for the emergence of fundamentalism;*

- ▶ *the characteristics of fundamentalism;*

- ▶ *the reasons why new religious movements originate;*

- ▶ *the characteristics of new religious movements.*

Secularisation

Aim

After studying this chapter you should be able to show knowledge and understanding of various definitions of religion and the six basic elements of secularisation. You should also be able to understand the contrasting evidence of the degree of secularisation in British society and be able to determine the extent of the influence of religion in contemporary society.

Secularisation is the name given to the decline in importance and influence of religion in society. The decline may appear obvious in some ways but there has been a lively debate over the issue since the 1960s.

If you want to know how many words there are on average on a page in this book, you first need to have a clear definition of what a word is. Do you count an abbreviation (such as e.g.) as a word? Does a number (e.g. 224,000) constitute one word? Do hyphenated words (such as inter-faith) count as one word or two? Before you can count or measure something, you need to have a clear and precise definition of what you are measuring. So it is with secularisation. Before you can determine the decline of religion in contemporary society, you must use a consistent and exact definition of religion

What is religion?

Task

Writing task	Write down in a sentence and in your own words a definition of religion. Compare yours with others in the group.
	Here are some definitions from those who have studied religion in society.
	[Place each definition in a separate box with comments on the definition outside the box]

"An expression in one form or another of a sense of dependence on a power outside ourselves, a power of which we may speak as a spiritual or moral power"
(Radcliffe-Brown)

Almost all religions have a belief in a Being or Beings who are powerful. Is belief in God or Gods essential for something to be a religion? Is it possible to be religious without believing in God? It is interesting that Buddhism is regarded as one of the world's six main religions yet the vast majority of Buddhists do not believe in any deity.

"The feelings, acts and experiences of individual men in their solitude, so far as they apprehend themselves to stand in relation to whatever they consider the divine"
(William James)

In this definition the word 'men' is used generically to mean both men and women and the word 'divine' is not necessarily limited to a Divine Being. This definition could certainly include Buddhists and Scientologists. The emphasis is on personal experience and individual understanding. Yet is religion no more than just an individual response?

"An attempt to formulate an all-embracing system of meaning"
(Berger and Luckmann)

It is true that all religions seek to explore the meaning of life and try to offer explanations as to why we are here and why life is as it is. However, such a broad definition could include Marxists and those whose philosophy of life is anti-religion and who would not want to be labelled 'religious'.

"A set of symbolic forms and acts which relate man to the ultimate condition of his existence" **(Bellah)**

This definition stresses ritual aspects. It is true that ceremonies, rites of passage and services of worship often form an important part of religion but there is far more to religion than symbolic actions.

"A unified system of beliefs and practices relative to sacred things . . . which unite into one moral unity, called a church, all those who adhere to them"
(Durkheim)

Whilst acknowledging that religion is a combination of both beliefs and practices, this understanding of religion is not only Christianity-orientated but emphasises the formal, social and institutional aspects. It raises the question as to whether a person has to belong to a religious community in order to be religious.

A phenomenon with a number of distinctive *"core dimensions – beliefs, practices, experiences, knowledge and consequences"*
(Glock and Stark)

This definition reflects the complexity of religion. Beliefs are doctrines; practices involve worship, prayer and ritual; experiences include feelings of awe and wonder and perceived direct encounters with the supernatural; knowledge is information such as religious stories; and consequences refers to moral and social behaviour.

Sociologists do not agree on what religion is. Some definitions are broader, vaguer and more inclusive than others. Some regard religious institutions, communities and ritual as what best constitutes religion, whilst others treat religion primarily in terms of belief and experiences.

Seminar topic

What are the likely consequences of there being no generally accepted definition of religion when debating secularisation?

Seminar topic

Do you need to believe in God or Gods to be religious?

Ready for conversion?

What is secularisation?

As with the definition of religion, the concept of secularisation is not without its problems. Whilst it is clearly to do with religion's apparent loss of importance and relevance, different sociologists seem to understand the issue in diverse ways. A range of meanings has been identified, as follows:

- the reduction in influence of religious institutions, doctrines and symbols;

- increasing concern with the present materialistic world;

- the separation of religious values from national and political life;

- the source of knowledge and motivation of behaviour being no longer grounded in religion;

- the centrality of humanity, nature and reason at the expense of the sacred and spiritual;

- general acceptance of a change from a sacred society to a secular one.

Three further problems with examining secularisation are:

- the extent of religious practice (such as attendance at religious services and rites of passage) can be measured, but not its significance – is someone who marries in a place of worship necessarily more religious than someone who marries elsewhere?

- evidence suggests that in contemporary society there may be little correlation between religious belief and religious practice – in the USA there are high rates of church attendance but lower rates of religious belief, whereas in the UK the opposite is true;

- the political organisation of a society can make it difficult to determine the true religiosity of a society – in a religious dictatorship such as Iran opposition to the state religion is not tolerated.

Measuring the extent of secularisation

Measuring the degree of secularisation involves comparing past societies with present ones. Secularisation is generally measured in terms of six indicators:

(i) decline in membership of and attendance at religious institutions;

(ii) reduction of religious influence in society;

(iii) growth of rational and scientific thought;

(iv) growth of religious pluralism;

(v) secularisation of religious institutions;

(vi) the emergence of mass media.

Whilst recognising that societies in other parts of the world may well be different, we will examine the extent of secularisation in our own society. Similarly, as it is only in the last thirty to forty years that religions other than Christianity have been much in evidence in our society, looking at Christianity is the best means for measuring secularisation.

(i) Decline in membership of and attendance at religious institutions

Increasingly fewer people in our society attend religious services. Within the Christian tradition, fewer people are baptised, confirmed and become active church members. The number of clergy has declined. A smaller proportion of the population gets married in a church, two-thirds opting for a non-religious civil ceremony. The percentage of the British population attending church at least once a week has dropped from about 35% at the beginning of the twentieth century, to 20% in 1950, 10% in 1970 and just over 6% in 2005. Church attendance in Wales declined by almost a fifth between 2001 and 2006, according to a recent report by the Church in Wales.

Summarise these charts in a sentence.

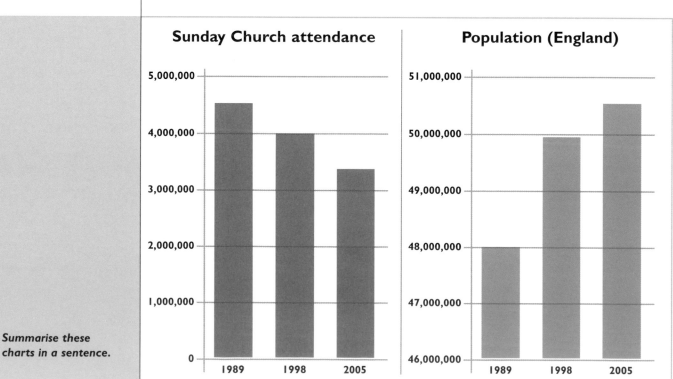

There are, however, several problems with such statistics:

- getting baptised and confirmed does not necessarily indicate that a person will practise a religious faith in adulthood;

- the major evidence of 19th Century religious practice is the 1851 Religious Census, but its figures need to be used with caution as they were based on church attendance on one particular Sunday and numbers at individual churches often appear to have been estimated;

- there are no commonly agreed criteria on which different Churches base their membership figures – for example, anyone baptised in a Roman Catholic church or attending mass regularly is counted as a member of that Church, but only those who have joined as an adult at a membership service are counted as members in the Methodist Church;

- at least some of the apparent decline in church attendance may simply reflect the fact that fewer people attend church twice on a Sunday;

- a decline in the numbers of those taking part in public worship does not necessarily indicate a decline in religious belief – in the past, attendance at religious services was more often out of duty, family pressure and social pressure than religious commitment and nowadays not attending any place of worship does not necessarily indicate that a person does not hold religious beliefs.

For reflection

Why in the past was there greater pressure to attend religious services?

(Clues: religion more part of accepted culture; family traditions/authority; chapels built by employers; church as hub of local social life).

Task

Research task	Find a set of recent statistics relating to religious activity in Wales or Britain. Present them as a chart or graph and indicate what they suggest regarding the state of religion in society.

(ii) Reduction of religious influence in society

There are many signs of the decrease of the influence of religion in society. There was a time when religious institutions throughout the world were the source of gaining an education, obtaining medical treatment and receiving relief from poverty. In Britain activities which are now part of local or national government were previously Church-dominated – particularly in the areas of education and social welfare. During the 20th Century the involvement of the Church was eroded by the development of democracy and political parties. Links between political parties and religion became increasingly either surreptitious or superficial – "we don't do God" declared an adviser of the former British Prime Minister Tony Blair. The Church has been relegated to the role of a pressure group. Clergy now have less status and their opinions are ignored by most people. Most people decide what is right and wrong according to their own conscience and feelings. Traditional religious teaching about the sanctity of marriage, the sanctity of life and the purpose of sex appears to have been largely ignored by a society which has facilitated easier and quicker divorce, given greater access to abortion and permitted lesbian and homosexual behaviour.

Seminar topic

Are there any arguments based on religious teachings which could be used to support our society's current laws on divorce, abortion and homosexuality?

Do religious schools divide a community?

But the influence of religion in society is far from extinguished. For example, the British Monarch remains the Defender of the Faith and Head of the Church of England, and bishops are much involved in the debates of the House of Lords. Many schools have religious foundations and new ones are still being opened. The number of pupils and students in schools and colleges taking Religious Studies as an examination subject, especially at GCSE, has increased substantially since 2000. Many individual religious communities remain heavily involved in social care activities – the Salvation Army is not alone in its practical care and compassion for the less fortunate people in society.

It can also be argued that reducing religion's political and material involvement in society may stimulate a renewed emphasis on spiritual concerns. Furthermore, religion's influence is more in individuals than in institutions. As the sociologist Talcott Parsons has observed, the real influence lies in 'the value-commitments and motivational commitments of individuals'. Most of us are more influenced by people we meet and like than by impersonal formal institutions and their creeds.

(iii) Growth of rational and scientific thought

Medieval Britain was characterised by a monolithic Catholic Church that had immense influence on both spiritual and secular aspects of life. Even when Protestantism emerged, biblical accounts of how the world began and of early history and Christian interpretations of the meaning of life were not seriously challenged. The seeds of rational thought were sown during the Renaissance in the 15th and 16th Centuries but only came to full fruition in the last half of the 19th Century.

Rational thought demands proof and logical reasons. This leads to a decline in acceptance of religious explanations based on the premise of a God or Gods. Similarly, as science increases understanding of the universe and human beings, the mysteries of life lessen and the need for anything supernatural decreases. Human problems are thought to be solved by rational thinking and scientific progress, not by prayer and religious ritual. The scientific and rational world-view is that life can be understandable and controllable.

Read and summarise a chapter of Dawkins' (pictured on the left) The God Delusion *and a chapter of McGrath's (pictured on the right)* The Dawkins Delusion.

On the other hand, neither rationalism nor science has generally satisfied people as to the origin of the universe and the meaning of life. Many people continue to think there is more to life than the physical and material. The popularity of horoscopes, prevalence of superstitions and involvement in 'fringe' religion (such as breakaway groups from traditional religions, new religious movements and the occult) are increasing not decreasing. Furthermore, science and religion, like reason and faith, are not necessarily incompatible. In fact many scientists and medical personnel, and some eminent philosophers, are religious believers, e.g. Sir Russell Stannard and John Polkinghorne.

(iv) Growth of religious pluralism

In a society where there is one exclusive or dominant religion, religious power and influence is strong. However, most modern societies are characterised by a large number of different religions, as well as non-religious world views such as Humanitarianism and Marxism. This is known as religious pluralism. This in itself diminishes the influence and authority of religion.

Competition reduces credibility. Where a religion is not perceived to have a monopoly of truth, it is no longer able to propagate a unique, unified and universally accepted set of beliefs and ideas. Not only is it impossible that all religions are right, but their conflicting claims and teachings cast doubt as to whether any of them are right.

However, religious beliefs persist strongly in contemporary society. Based on various polls conducted since the beginning of this century, around two-thirds of people in Britain say they believe in God. During the last fifty years there has been a proliferation of new religious movements and increasing congregations in a significant proportion of charismatic, evangelical and fundamentalist-type churches within Christianity. Other world religions have also expanded in Britain. For example, between 1980 and 2000 the number of Muslims in Britain doubled. Many new Buddhist communities have been established since the first Tibetan Buddhist centre was set up in Scotland in 1967. So some sociologists assert that religion in our society is in a state of change or transformation rather than of terminal decline.

For reflection

Can you think of ways in which science and reason have helped solve human problems or explain something?

Chapter 6

Task

| **Research task** | Find out the meaning of the terms (i) charismatic, (ii) evangelical and (iii) fundamentalist. |

(v) Secularisation of religious institutions

It is argued that during the last century there was an increasing tendency for churches to move from their traditional 'other world' emphasis (e.g. concerns about heaven/hell and salvation) to a 'this world' emphasis (e.g. concerns about social justice and health/wealth in this life). Traditional Christian doctrines and views on moral issues (e.g.

the virgin birth and resurrection of Jesus, and divorce) have been modified to comply with the changing ethos of society. More recently, new religious movements and newly-formed churches are run on a similar basis to secular businesses. Leaders use management techniques and advocate salesmen's 'hard sell' and 'soft sell' techniques to gain more members. Success seems to be measured in terms of the number of members or amount of money in the collections. Such change makes ordinary people suspicious and disillusioned with religious institutions.

It is debatable whether this argument is valid. The Church was far more involved in politics in earlier times, when many archbishops were as much statesmen as priests, than it has been for the last hundred years or so. The Church was also much involved in social reform in the early and mid 19th century before the process of secularisation is said to have started. Moreover, there has always been reassessment of doctrines and moral views within Christianity and other religions as understanding of sacred writings, religious traditions, science and humanity has developed. Similarly, using contemporary techniques indicates vitality not fossilisation! What worked in a previous generation does not necessarily work for the modern generation. That such changes alienate people from religion is unproven.

Seminar topic

To what extent should religious communities move with the times with regard to beliefs, worship and organisation?

(vi) The emergence of mass media

In a society without mass communications and mass education, religion is able to control how people interpret life. For centuries a local area depended on its churches, particular the parish church, for its news and social activities. Even in 19th Century Britain most people were not influenced by the media, as books and newspapers were mainly the preserve of the middle and upper classes. Today, though, the mass media are the main providers of information, opinion and experience.

Television in particular has become the major source of information and a major leisure activity. Not only are the news and opinions selective but also a variety of forms of entertainment are provided. Even religious programmes themselves can be substitutes for going to public worship – watching TV is more comfortable and it can be switched off if it becomes boring! Additionally, TV programmes and books which not only question religious beliefs but are hostile to religion, especially those which lack balance and discussion, undermine faith. Many viewers and readers may lack the knowledge and understanding to critically assess the arguments and therefore believe the stated opinions are proven facts.

Do these programmes increase or lessen apathy towards religious institutions?

There is no denying the strong influence of the media. If this were not so, commercial companies would not advertise on independent television channels and in newspapers. However, the influence may be exaggerated. Since the advent of the GCSEs in the mid-1980s, young people have been encouraged to assess and analyse information. More educated viewers and readers are less likely to accept opinions without clear-cut evidence. Also watching a box is no substitute for social interaction with like-minded people, which is what public worship offers. Additionally, some religious movements are increasingly using visual media to propagate their teachings and views.

There has been a drift away from organised traditional religion in Britain. However, now that attending a place of worship is not required to be seen as respectable or for any other social reason, it may be that those who went a hundred or more years ago for purely religious reasons are no greater numerically than those who go today. Religious belief appears to remain strong. The growing number of independent Christian churches, new religious movements and non-Christian places of worship in Britain might indeed suggest that there are as many committed religious believers in Britain as ever.

Task

| Writing task | (a) Explain what is meant by 'secularisation'. |
| | (b) Is religion declining or reviving in contemporary British society? |

Glossary

correlation	Relation between two or more things
monolithic	Uniform; only one
religiosity	Being religious
sacred	Dedicated to a god or to some religious purpose; set apart or made holy by religious association
sanctity	Specialness of something; not to be damaged or violated
secular	Concerned with things of this world; not spiritual or religious

Fundamentalism

Aim

After studying this chapter you should be able to show knowledge and understanding of the causes and characteristics of religious fundamentalism. You should also be able to understand the strengths and weaknesses of fundamentalism and be able to assess its likely impact on religion in Britain in the future.

Fundamentalism is to be found within every major religious tradition. Basically, this is a conservative world view that highlights what is regarded as essential truths of a traditional faith and applies them with fervour to the contemporary situation. It seeks to promote – and sometimes impose – what is regarded as 'The Truth' on a pluralistic and complex world. Many see the emergence of a militant form of fundamentalism in many religious traditions over the past 30 years as particularly alarming, especially when it has been linked to events such as the 9/11 attack on the Twin Towers in New York in 2001 and the 7/7 bombings in London in 2005. But, it must be remembered that the term 'fundamentalism' describes a much broader spectrum of religious experience than the militant groups which grab our attention through the popular press: these represent only one aspect of this complex phenomenon.

Origins of the term

Fundamentalism is not a new concept. Its roots go back to the mid-18th Century when British and American Christian preachers delivered powerful sermons describing the horrors of Hell based on a literal understanding of the biblical text. However, the term 'fundamentalism' only emerged in the 1920s, to describe American Protestant Christians who affirmed certain beliefs as the 'fundamentals' of faith.

In 1910 a series of religious pamphlets began to be published by a group of American and British theologians called *The Fundamentals: A Testimony of Truth*. They were aimed at promoting what the writers regarded as the essential basic beliefs of Christianity:

- the inerrancy (freedom from error) of the Bible;

- the creation of the universe by God;

- the reality of miracles, including Jesus' virgin birth and resurrection;

- the substitutionary atonement of Christ (that Jesus' death paid the price for the sins of humanity);

- the Second Coming of Christ.

Fundamentalists were those who accepted *The Fundamentals*.

Seminar topic

Do you think all these five beliefs are essential in order to be a Christian?

Dr. Barry Morgan, Archbishop of Wales

Causes of fundamentalism

All forms of fundamentalism have emerged as a response to a perceived threat against religious belief. By the end of the 19th Century there were Christians, Jews and Muslims who believed that their faith was under attack. This fear increased during the 20th Century and became more widespread within these three religions and extended to other world faiths too, although until the 1970s the term 'fundamentalism' was generally confined to Christianity.

As transport and worldwide communication became universally available and accessible, people became more aware of the vast range of existing religious, cultural and social differences. Previously there had been an assumption that one's own way of life and beliefs were the norm, but now this idea was challenged.

The perceived threat to religious belief was three-fold:

- textual criticism of sacred writings;

- general acceptance of scientific explanations of life;

- increasing influence of secular authority.

(i) Textual criticism

From the mid-19th Century onwards, new methods of textual analysis of the Bible became common. Repetitions, apparent inconsistencies, alleged contradictions and different writing styles within the same document were discovered. As a result, strong doubts were expressed about previously accepted traditions (such as Moses being the author of the Pentateuch, the first five Books of the Old Testament, and the whole of the Book of Isaiah being written by one prophet of that name). Textual criticism of the New Testament, which questioned its traditional authorship and historical accuracy, was particularly hard for some Christians to accept.

The reaction of those Christians who felt threatened by such liberal ideas, was to reject all scholarly criticism of the Bible. What made it worse for them was that other

Christian believers were willing to accept and adopt these disturbing ideas. So the threat came from both outside and inside their religion.

Some Jewish fundamentalists reacted similarly and began to observe the 613 laws in the Torah more stringently than ever before. Islam has been relatively untouched by textual criticism of the Qur'an: critical analysis is not permitted. Anyone casting doubt on its authenticity or accuracy is still likely to be deemed a blasphemer.

(ii) Scientific explanations

One of the threats to religious belief in the minds of Christian fundamentalists was the rise of evolutionary thinking. This began with the publication of Charles Darwin's *The Origin of Species* in 1859, which undermined belief in a 6,000-year-old world and a six-day creation. By the end of the 19th Century, the concept of evolution had become more widely accepted and extended to explain social behaviour and even religious belief itself.

The reaction of fundamentalists was to reject any scientific theories or discoveries which seemed to conflict with statements in the stories in the early chapters of the Book of Genesis. In 1925, in what became known as the 'Monkey Trial', instigated by pressure from American fundamentalists, a secondary school science teacher called John Scopes was prosecuted and fined in Tennessee for teaching evolution.

A satirical question on the evolution debate in a cartoon from Punch, 1861

(iii) Secular authority

Religion played a significant and sometimes dominant role in the government of many nations until about 150 years ago. With the emergence of new scientific and rational ideas, as well as new political ideologies such as Marxism, that role lessened considerably. In addition, society has changed at an increasing rate over the past fifty or so years. Such changes have made some religious believers feel not only anxious and bewildered but also insecure and threatened.

For Jewish and Muslim fundamentalists the main issue was, and is, more about society's values than about sacred writings. In countries where secular authority governs, tolerance rather than religious truth is more important. Fundamentalism is a response to anxieties that society tolerates ways and beliefs which are radically different from those understood by religious believers to be God-given.

So observance of scriptural laws in a secular society is the paramount concern for Jews and Muslims. Most, but not all, Jewish fundamentalists (such as the Jewish settler movement Gush Emunim) have tended to want Israel to be a religious state and interpret the Arab-Israeli conflict in terms of defending God's land against God's enemies. Many Muslim fundamentalists have regarded Western imperialism (European occupation of non-European land) and modernity as undermining Islamic traditions; some not only call for a 'Holy War' against non-Muslims as an expression of 'Jihad', but also want countries to be governed according to what they believe to be God-given Shari'a law.

Task

Research task   Research the various interpretations of 'jihad' within Islam.

There have also been Hindu, Sikh, Buddhist and even Confucian fundamentalists who have aimed to defend the purity of their land and/or culture, rejected many values of the society in which they lived and fought and killed in the name of religion. For example, Buddhist fundamentalists in Sri Lanka first fought against Western colonialism and more recently against Hindu Tamils.

Characteristics of fundamentalism

The Fundamentalism Project, based at the University of Chicago between 1988 and 1993, identified nine characteristics of fundamentalists. Since the nature of fundamentalism varies from one religion to another, some religious groups stressing behaviour rather than belief, not all nine characteristics are found in any one group. The nine characteristics are:

(i)   reactivity to the marginalisation of religion;

(ii)   selectivity;

(iii)   moral dualism;

(iv)   absolutism and inerrancy;

(v)   millennialism and messianism;

(vi)   elect membership;

(vii)   sharp boundaries;

(viii) authoritarian leadership;

(ix)   behavioural requirements.

(i) Reactivity to the marginalisation of religion

The importance of religion in many societies is declining. This can be seen in contemporary preoccupation with self and material things – money, possessions, power, status, celebrity and so on. It is also evident in common questioning and rejecting of traditional values and general acceptance of relativism (the idea that religion is culturally bound and only relatively true or false). All this leads fundamentalists to the conviction that true faith is being eroded by modern thinking and is under attack.

Some fundamentalists react defensively by withdrawing from society: the Amish, for example, are content living isolated in their own communities in the United States and Canada. Others react by parading their distinctiveness in society by the particular way they dress or behave. Some seek to influence society by their involvement in local issues or in politics - one example of the latter is the so-called Moral Majority movement in the USA, which helped George Bush get elected as President of that country in the 1990s. Yet others react militantly by trying to limit or suppress those who think differently from them. This is evident in clashes between Hindus and Muslims in India and between Sinhala Buddhists and Hindu Tamils in Sri Lanka.

Seminar topic

Can violence ever be justified in defending or promoting a faith?

The Amish live in their own community and preserve the dress and lifestyle of the late 17th Century.

(ii) Selectivity

Fundamentalists tend to select and stress particular aspects of their religion. Certain parts of their sacred writings or religious traditions are emphasised and others ignored. This is most clearly seen in their use of sacred texts when considering moral issues. For example, Jewish and Protestant fundamentalists frequently quote the first part of Leviticus 20:13 when condemning homosexuality. This states that homosexuality is 'detestable' to God. However, they rarely quote the second part of the verse which demands the death penalty for such activity or support another demand in that chapter – the death penalty for children who curse their parents. Similarly, extreme Muslim fundamentalists can justify violent actions by interpreting the 'Sword' verses in the Qur'an as a call to kill non-Muslims rather than as spiritual guidance against evil and ignoring other texts such as 'slay not the life that Allah has made sacred'.

Task

Research task	Use the Internet to find out what the 'Sword' verses are and how they are interpreted in different ways.

Fundamentalists also often select certain issues to focus on. For example, abortion and evolution, the tourist trade in Egypt and the surrender of 'land for peace' in Israel, are singled out for special opposition by some Christians, Muslims and Jews respectively.

(iii) Moral dualism

Dualism is a world view in which there is a clear division between good and evil, right and wrong. Fundamentalists regard the world as contaminated, sinful and doomed. The only hope of salvation is through the movement of which they are part.

Other world religions are regarded as inferior, if not evil, and alternative expressions of faith within their own religion as misguided and misleading, if not heretical and blasphemous. Those who are not part of their belief system are part of the evil world. For extremist Shi'ite Muslims, for example, secularised Shi'ite Muslims, compromising Sunni Muslims and non-Muslims all oppose the will of Allah.

(iv) Absolutism and inerrancy

Fundamentalists have a need and desire for certainty. Their beliefs and concepts are absolute, unconditional and non-negotiable. They are intolerant of religious diversity, as they believe theirs is the only true faith. Similarly, they deal in moral absolutes. For them, moral issues are clear-cut and an action is either right or wrong, regardless of the situation.

Their sacred writings are regarded by fundamentalists as being of divine origin, true and accurate in every respect. Fundamentalists tend to favour an historical and literal interpretation of their scriptures rather than a metaphorical or symbolic one. In some cases not only the sacred text but also traditional interpretations and applications (such as the Talmud for Jews and Shari'a law for Muslims) are held as also being without error. Since such writings and traditions are regarded as absolute truth, fundamentalists usually oppose contemporary critical methods of examining religious sources and reject the conclusions of modern scholars.

In Buddhism and Hinduism, authority tends to lie with fundamental traditions taught by individual gurus, monks or priests, such as Anagarika Dharmapala and Shankayracharya of Puri, rather than with any sacred text. These individuals are perceived by their followers to be divinely inspired or to have special enlightened understanding. Consequently their pronouncements are to be accepted and not questioned.

In short, the idea that that there are equally valid, diverse interpretations of a sacred text or equally weighty arguments for conflicting views is rejected.

Seminar topic

What are the benefits and problems in basing one's beliefs on a sacred book or a religious leader?

(v) Millennialism and messianism

Millennial expectations are another characteristic of fundamentalist movements. Fundamentalists share a conviction that ultimately good will triumph over evil. This world will end and God, the Ultimate Being or Enlightenment, will prevail.

This is most evident in Christian, Islamic and Jewish fundamentalist movements. For example, the Saviour, Hidden Imam or Messiah will come and usher in a new age where sin and suffering no longer exist. The expected outcome for Hindu fundamentalist movements and the Sinhala Buddhists are nations protected from alien influences, but concepts of the Kingdom of Ram, Khalistan and the purely Buddhist 'kingdom' of Sri Lanka have millennial overtones.

Task

Research task	Find out more about one of the six concepts mentioned in the above paragraph and prepare a two-minute presentation on it for the rest of the group.

(vi) Elect membership

Many fundamentalists think of themselves as chosen people, the elect. They may be chosen in the sense of being called by God to be a witness to the truth. Or they may be chosen to carry out certain tasks required by God. The most dreadful act of violence by extreme fundamentalists in recent times is probably the hijacking of four aircraft by Islamic militants on September 11th 2001. They belonged to the al-Qaeda movement led by Osama bin Laden and at least some of the hijackers clearly believed they had been chosen by Allah to defend the true faith.

(vii) Sharp boundaries

Clear separation between believers and unbelievers, the saved and the unsaved, is general among fundamentalist movements. Usually the movement has a rigid set of beliefs which have to be accepted by members and this belief system itself marks out the true believer from the rest of humanity.

The 9/11 attack when over 3,000 people were killed and thousands of others physically or mentally scarred

Separation may be physical in the sense in which the ultra-Orthodox Haredi Jews require their members to live within easy walking distance of their synagogue and demand that their social life is organised around the talmud Torah (school), synagogue, kosher slaughterhouse and the mikva (ritual bath). Or it could be in the setting up of a separate closed community, as in the case of the Amish.

More usual is separation within society by practice and witness – 'in the world but not of it'. For example, many Christian fundamentalist groups run schools where their children are taught a Bible-based curriculum that rejects the findings of modern science that conflict with their faith, such as beliefs concerning the origins of the universe.

(viii) Authoritarian leadership

Many a fundamentalist group is led by a charismatic individual (usually male) who, with a few trusted followers, makes all the important decisions. Questioning such decisions is not tolerated. His interpretation of sacred writings or religious traditions, moral and political pronouncements and family and financial decisions are implemented.

Seminar topic

What qualities do you think are needed to be a charismatic leader?

The leader is set apart from all others and is revered. This can be seen in rituals, such as touching the prayer garment of the Jewish rebbe and kissing the hand of the Muslim Jama'a emir. It may be seen in the repeated reading of the writings of the leader, as with the 'Mo Letters' of Moses David Berg, leader of the Children of God (now called the Family). It is also evident in the avid listening to the leader's long and frequent sermons and speeches, as with the followers of David Koresh, leader of the Branch Davidian until the destruction of the community at Waco, Texas, in 1993.

(ix) Behavioural requirements

Conforming to certain behaviour is also characteristic of fundamentalists. Often this includes not only moral conduct but also family relationships and spiritual duties. Sometimes there is even a dress code, such as the shorts and lathis (staves) for members of the Hindu Shakhas and the black coat and hat for the Jewish Haredim.

Behaviour which is regarded as wrong is condemned. Any who do not conform are called to account before their leader and sometimes fellow-believers and, if remorse, repentance and reform are not apparent, they are excluded from the group.

Strengths and weaknesses

Fundamentalism is a complex phenomenon. It not only takes different forms from one religion to another but is expressed differently by fundamentalist movements within the same religion. Most religious fundamentalists are law-abiding and peaceful people and militant extremists are a small minority.

Task

Research task

Research at least 3 fundamentalist movements from EITHER Christianity OR Islam: state which are law-abiding and peaceful, and which are militant and extremist.
Give reasons to support your answer.

Those who hold fundamentalist beliefs have strong convictions, unshakeable faith and often great courage. They hold fast to what they believe is truth and have a confidence which comes from the certainty of their convictions. They are sincere, have a strong sense of community and usually embrace a strict morality.

Fundamentalism is a protest against the materialistic and selfish values and ways of life which dominate society today and is a wake-up call to take spiritual aspects and the fundamental questions of life seriously.

On the other hand, some fundamentalists can be intolerant and arrogant, lacking warmth and compassion for those who do not share their beliefs. This intolerance is normally expressed verbally, but militant groups are prepared to turn to violent action in order to defend what they regard as 'the truth'.

Critics of fundamentalism would argue that many of the issues they concentrate on, such as evolution and 'purification' of their land, seem trivial compared to global issues of poverty, injustice and environmental pollution. Fundamentalism is also usually patriarchal and often misogynist. In other words, male leadership is the norm and the role of women is limited and subordinate.

Most fundamentalists see everything in black and white terms: they do not accept that there are grey areas. Different groups within a religion select and stress different religious traditions or texts and yet fundamentalists claim that their particular version of faith is a return to the original, authentic religion. Christian fundamentalists in particular use their sacred writing as an information manual and take texts out of context, sometimes as a pretext for justifying a predetermined attitude or course of action.

There is evidence that religious fundamentalism in Britain is increasing. This can be seen in the growth of fundamentalist churches and mosques, increasing fundamentalist use of television and the Internet, the amount of fundamentalist literature being published and even the involvement of fundamentalists in the setting up of school academies. Whilst the majority of fundamentalists are law-abiding and peaceful, some are more militant, and have expressed their fundamentalism through terrorism.

How much further fundamentalism will influence and impact on religion in Britain is speculation, but one thing is certain: fundamentalism is not going to disappear.

Task

Writing task	(a) Explain why it is difficult to define what a fundamentalist is.
	(b) "The strengths of fundamentalism outweigh its weaknesses." Assess this view.

Glossary

emir	A Muslim ruler
Marxism	Political and economic theories of Karl Marx; the ideology of a classless, anti-capitalistic, communist society
modernity	State of being contemporary or in current fashion
pluralistic	Acceptance of a number of different religions and religious groups
rebbe	Rabbi in Chasidic ('pious') Judaism
Shari'a	Muslim code of religious law
textual criticism	Process of attempting to determine the correct reading of a text
Torah	The Pentateuch (first five books of the Tenakh/Old Testament); Jewish Law

New religious movements

Aim

After studying this chapter you should be able to show knowledge and understanding of the causes and characteristics of new religious movements. You should also be able to understand the relative significance of these causes to the emergence of new religious movements and be able to assess the likely impact of such movements on religion in Britain in the future.

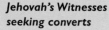
Jehovah's Witnesses seeking converts

Religion is never static. New experiences, new emphases and breakaway movements from traditional religion are part of the process of religion remaining relevant in a changing society. Whilst the emergence and existence of new religious movements is not a new phenomenon, there has been an unprecedented proliferation of such movements during the last 150 years, particularly from the 1950s onwards.

The term 'new religious movements' is used by some scholars to refer only to those religious organisations that have originated since the mid-1940s. However, such a definition would exclude groups like the Watchtower Tract Society (Jehovah's Witnesses), the Church of Jesus Christ of Latter-Day Saints (Mormons), the Lubavitch Movement, the Baha'i Faith and the Meher Baba Movement, which remain significant international religious movements today.

The nature of new religious movements

New religious movements are a complex phenomenon to study. This is because they can be so essentially different from each other. Many are variations of an established religion – some opposing change, some championing particular teachings which may once have been believed but since abandoned, and others seeking to incorporate new teachings into the religion. Other movements are a mixing of religious traditions and yet others an attempt to find a new sense of the Divine.

It is therefore not surprising that the factors leading to the emergence of a new religious movement vary from movement to movement. Similarly, the elements of what comprises a new religious movement differ enormously.

Some new religious movements exist for barely a generation, whilst others exist for centuries. Some become part of established religion (Methodism is a case in point), whilst others remain regarded as a fringe religion (such as the Jehovah's Witnesses).

Seminar topic

Why do you think some new religious movements last for so long but continue to be regarded by traditional religion and society in general as fringe religion?

Causes of new religious movements

There are a number of possible causes to explain the origin and development of new religious movements. It may well be that some causes are more pertinent to certain movements and others to different movements.

The possible causes are:

(i) disillusionment with established religion;

(ii) a sense of disadvantage or deprivation;

(iii) social change;

(iv) a reaction to a secular society;

(v) contemporary emphasis on self;

(vi) emergence of charismatic leadership.

(i) Disillusionment with established religion

Well-established religious organisations seem to lose some of their original dynamism and vitality. There is a tendency to compromise beliefs and attitudes and become more integrated into wider society. As a result, some members feel that the organisation, community or movement is no longer being faithful to its original views and values. So these members break away and form their own independent religious organisation.

Examples of such breakaway groups include Kimbanguism in Africa and the Jewish Havurot movement. However, there are clearly some new religious movements which were created by those outside established religion, such as Scientology and Eckanker.

(ii) A sense of disadvantage or deprivation

A number of sociologists have suggested that new forms of religion are likely to emerge amongst those who are in the lower social groups in society. Weber, for example, argued that such people need an explanation for why they are in their social position and an alternative sense of superiority over others. New religious movements usually offer what he terms 'a theodicy of disprivilege', (a religious explanation for why some people are socially disadvantaged) by declaring the world as corrupt and affirming members as an elite.

Similarly, Niebuhr and Troeltsch believed that new religious movements arise from situations of material poverty. Glock and Stark have pointed out that deprivation may be in forms other than economic. People can feel disadvantaged by such things as lack of status, disability and chronic ill-health, having no prospects of bettering themselves and being without a meaningful value system. Whatever the source of their deprivation, people create or join movements that help them alleviate their deprivation.

For reflection

Karl Marx said, "religion is the opium of the people". How might this second reason be used to argue that religion is a drug to mask people's suffering?

A sense of disadvantage or deprivation would appear to be an important element in the origins of some new religious groups such as the Rastafarian and Black Muslim movements. Similarly, many who joined the Branch Davidians and Peoples Temple were black and working class. However, far more people who join other new religious movements are clearly not deprived or do not feel deprived prior to their involvement. Scientology, for example, appears to attract mainly confident, prosperous and articulate people, including some well-established celebrities.

Chapter 8

Task

Research task — Choose one of the movements mentioned in (i) or (ii) and find out how it originated and what its main features are. Prepare a three-minute presentation or handout of your findings.

(iii) Social change

Other sociologists such as Wilson believe that new forms of religion develop in conditions of rapid social change which disrupt normal life. The rise of Methodism in 18th Century England and Wales, for instance, is seen as a response by workers to the disruption and uncertainty of life in new industrial areas. Similarly, the constant changes in contemporary society during the past fifty years or so are seen as ideal conditions for the founding of new religious movements. Such movements offer a sense of belonging, strong community ties, support, stability and purpose when everything else seems to be unreliable and unstable.

John Wesley, the Anglican clergyman who founded Methodism, preaching

Another relevant aspect of social change is the emergence of societies which are multi-cultural. For various reasons people born in one culture have increasingly emigrated to live in a different culture. They bring with them different traditions, ideas and beliefs, so no longer is there one exclusive religion in a country. Religious pluralism is a fact of life and new religious movements fit in with the concept of alternative forms of religion and spirituality within society.

In addition, the mass media inform and promote diversity of belief. Through literature, radio, television and the Internet, information about different cultures and religious beliefs has become increasingly available and more widely known. Indeed, with the advent of satellite and cable television, more and more religious organisations promote themselves by such means.

(iv) A reaction to secular society

Sorokin, another sociologist, saw the culture of society as a sort of pendulum which swings slowly between the extremes of materialism and spirituality. He regarded new religious forms as a reaction to the extreme of a secular, materialistic society, a response to a world dominated by the technical, scientific, rational and impersonal.

For reflection

To which extreme do you think the pendulum is swinging in our society today?

Why?

Certainly the 1960s were a time of affluence in Britain and the USA and it was in that decade that many new religious movements began. A counter-culture came into being which included hippies, 'flower people' and 'soft' drugs, but it was also the time when Western Zen groups, Hindu religious movements such as the Divine Light Mission and other new religious organisations emerged. Many of these new religious movements adopted a simple and ascetic life-style and attracted the young and relatively affluent.

(v) Contemporary emphasis on self

In contemporary society there is an increased emphasis on personal fulfilment, happiness and finding one's own moral values. The old pattern of authority that used to prevail is increasingly redundant and the idea of each individual making up his/her own mind within a range of choice is the ideal in our contemporary society.

It is hardly surprising, therefore, that some people experiment with different forms of spirituality, in the same way as some move from job to job or change cars they drive. Individuals can choose their own spiritual path and decide what, in their view, is true and useful. New religious movements fit in with this scheme of things

Seminar topic

Members of the Oshu movement gain enlightenment through music, singing, dancing and meditation. Do you think these activities alone are adequate for spiritual development?

Members of the Oshu movement meditating

(vi) Emergence of charismatic leadership

Most religions have a founder who is considered to possess extraordinary powers or gifts. The vast majority of new religious movements also are founded by individuals who have attractive personalities, dynamic energy and exceptional powers of persuasion. Classic examples of groups that are formed by and around a charismatic leader are the Family Federation for World Peace and Unification (Moonies) formed by Sun Myung Moon and ISKCON (the Hare Krishna movement) formed by the Indian guru Swami Prabhupada.

Types of new religious movements

There have been several attempts to categorise new religious movements into various types with varying success. The problem is that it is hard to generalise about such movements because they are so different in origin, nature, practices and beliefs. Perhaps the most helpful distinction between new religious movements is based on their general attitude to the world at large. Some are essentially world-rejecting, some world-affirming and others world-accommodating.

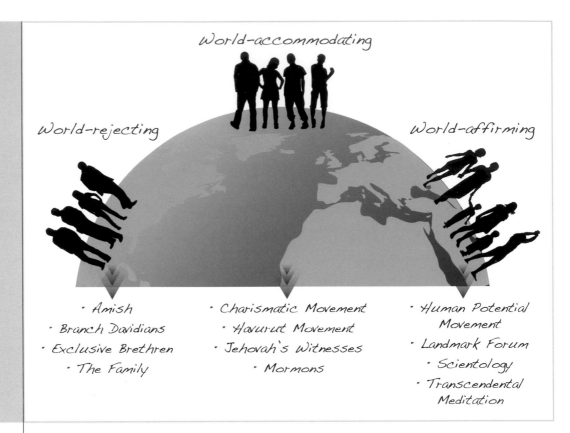

World-accommodating

World-rejecting

World-affirming

- Amish
- Branch Davidians
- Exclusive Brethren
- The Family

- Charismatic Movement
- Havurut Movement
- Jehovah's Witnesses
- Mormons

- Human Potential Movement
- Landmark Forum
- Scientology
- Transcendental Meditation

Types of New Religious Movements

a) World-rejecting

Some movements regard contemporary society as corrupt, needing to be entirely abandoned or wholly transformed. The world is considered so evil that the only way to honour God and live out a godly life is to be separate from society, either by living in community with like-minded believers in total isolation or by spending one's life serving the movement, worshipping, working and evangelising.

Leaders are venerated as special messengers from God and their teachings accepted and instructions obeyed without question. There tends to be a rigid belief-system and a clear-cut moral code. Commitment and loyalty to the movement is paramount.

b) World-affirming

Other movements accept most of the values and goals of contemporary society. The world is seen as having many good features and it is believed society benefits when individuals are enabled to bring out their full potential. There is more emphasis on techniques and individual attainment in terms of understanding, happiness and relationships than on dogmatic and detailed beliefs.

Leaders are respected but not revered. Living in community and full-time commitment is not demanded but financial support in the form of donations or set fees is expected. Members normally continue with conventional lifestyles, careers and family life.

c) World-accommodating

Some movements neither fully accept nor wholly reject the values of contemporary society. It is thought that the world in general and religion in particular has moved away from encouraging the sort of life God ordained and that society needs religious revival by individuals experiencing spiritual renewal.

Leadership tends to be shared and is regarded more as a service than a privilege. The emphasis is on personal and shared spiritual growth. Members' external lifestyle is usually conventional. Co-operation with other religious groups often occurs and sometimes those in the movement even remain within an established religious institution.

Religious movements often change over the years and may move gradually away from one type to another. For example, the Church of Jesus Christ of Latter-Day Saints, ISKCON and the Family Federation for World Peace and Unification were originally in the world-rejecting category, but are now more accurately in the world-accommodating one. Even some of the Amish now have interaction with their local communities and sell goods directly to tourists. What is important to note is that the categorical type determines which characteristics are paramount in a movement.

Characteristics of new religious movements

Each new religious movement exhibits the following characteristics in varying degrees and one or two of them hardly at all. Differences in attitude to society and conventional life have already been considered but there is also a huge variation in their concept of what is true and what is Divine. The characteristics below distinguish such movements from traditional and established forms of religion.

1. **It is essentially a protest group.** The protest may be against the loss of vitality in established religion, or against secular society or the current values and expectations of the State. This protest can involve not only antagonism to at least some beliefs, values and institutions of contemporary life but also opposition to some laws (such as those concerning taxes, conscription and voting). There is a tendency to ignore or avoid involvement in the state system of the country in which they live. Political systems, state organisations and government agencies are regarded as irrelevant at best and downright evil at worst.

Falun Gong members protesting in Beijing in 1999 before being banned by the Chinese government

2. **Many of its beliefs, practices and values are rejected by society.** The degree of hostility is most marked towards world-rejecting movements, but all are treated with some suspicion. New religious movements arouse rejection because they form a variant sub-culture within society, challenging its norms and sometimes threatening its values. Such movements are not represented at any state or official occasions.

3. **It claims to have either a monopoly of the whole truth or exclusive insight into some aspects of life.** The truest way, the best way or the most godly way of living is through the movement. Only its members are 'the elect', the 'saved' or reach the full potential of their humanity. Other religious groups are deluded, deviant or devilish.

4. **Some beliefs and teachings are never publicly proclaimed or discussed.** There is a body of special or secret knowledge which is confined to members of the movement or only divulged gradually as the member progresses through stages of commitment. Such restricted access avoids critical examination of and group challenges to controversial beliefs and teachings.

5. **It is founded and led by a charismatic individual who often is regarded as special in one way or another.** Any other leadership within the movement is mainly, if not exclusively, lay and unpaid. In other words, there is no concept of certain people being set apart as 'professional priests'.

6. **It differs from traditional religions by recruiting members mainly by conversion.** It rejects established orthodox sacraments, minimises ritual and tends to have a form of worship which is intense, expressive and includes passionate and prolonged teaching. It also often puts greater emphasis on a dramatic future (such as the Second Coming of Christ, Armageddon) than on past or present events.

7. **The movement exercises strict control over its members.** This includes tests of entry and expulsion for those who do not conform. Those in full membership are expected to be fully committed to the movement, conforming to all rules of behaviour, accepting all beliefs without question and attending all required spiritual activities. Freedom of thought is minimal and individuality is often suppressed for the sake of the community.

Seminar topic

How do the characteristics of a new religious movement differ from those of established, traditional, orthodox religion?

The future of new religious movements

There is no reason to doubt that new religious movements will continue to be formed and develop in the future. The factors which have led in the past to the emergence of such movements are likely to continue. The causes identified earlier in this chapter are unlikely to disappear.

The needs of different groups, such as the culturally deprived, the socially disadvantaged, ethnic minorities and those disillusioned with established religion, are likely to remain a catalyst for the emergence of new religious movements. The search for the meaning of life and for spiritual fulfilment, combined with the rise of charismatic individuals, is part of human nature. How numerous and attractive such movements will be in the future depends much on the state of society and the state of established religions at any one time.

What is clear is that, as in the past, religious movements emerge, develop and change or disappear. Over time most world-rejecting movements either become less hostile and more conventional or dwindle until they cease to exist. World-affirming movements tend to modify according to the prevailing culture or be replaced by completely new movements which better fit into prevailing thinking.

In short, new religious movements are a phenomenon which is likely to persist as one form of religious expression in the foreseeable future.

Task

Writing task	(a) Outline the distinctive features of new religious movements.
	(b) "The large number of new religious movements in contemporary society is due to so many people feeling deprived and disadvantaged."
	Assess this view.

Seminar topic

Are new religious movements beneficial for (a) religion and (b) society?

Glossary

ascetic	Self-disciplined and frugal; abstaining from pleasure
conversion	Process of changing belief(s); experience of a convert
elite	Select group
guru	Spiritual or religious leader, usually Hindu
lay	having a position in an organisation, especially a religious one, that is not full-time and is not paid
sub-culture	Group with beliefs and practices at variance with those generally accepted as normal by the society in which they live
theodicy	Argument showing how the existence of God is compatible with the existence of suffering and evil

Religion and the Individual

Aim of the section

This section asks you to consider the contribution made to the study of religion by two key psychologists, Sigmund Freud and Carl Jung. It also asks that you reflect on the value of a psychological approach to the study of religion.

This means you will have to consider the following key matters:

▶ *the nature of the psychology of religion compared with other disciplines, such as the sociology of religion;*

▶ *the debate about whether practising and believing in religion is either healthy or neurotic;*

▶ *the notion of the unconscious mind as the true source of religion;*

▶ *the role of both dreams and religious narrative in illuminating the unconscious mind;*

▶ *Freud's concepts of repression, projection, negation, illusion and maturity as they relate to religion;*

▶ *Jung's concepts of the collective unconscious, the archetypes, myth, symbol and individuation as they relate to religion;*

▶ *Freud and Jung's contrasting evaluation of the role of religion in psychological health.*

Freud

Aim

After studying this chapter, you will have been introduced to Freud's understanding of religion, and engaged with it critically.

In Section 3 of this text, you studied the ways in which religion and society are understood to relate to each other. This section focuses on the individual. A famous definition of religion offered by A N Whitehead states that 'Religion is what a man does with his own solitariness.' Of course, when Whitehead said 'a man' he meant people in general. Certainly, it makes sense to see religion as a personal activity, even a private one, often focused on 'the inner life', and on thoughts and feelings.

Sociological theories about religions often leave that dimension of religion out, preferring to look at community activities and rituals, but for many people in the modern world religion is about private beliefs, attitudes and choices.   Using psychology alongside sociology in the study of religion helps to redress the balance, and puts the individual nearer to the centre of concern.

The psychology of religion is a very wide field (and psychology in general much wider!). In this section of the book, you will be focusing on two psychologists only: Sigmund Freud (1858-1939) and Carl Jung (1875-1961).

These two men knew each other, and in fact Jung had been a disciple of Freud. They shared many theories in common. They both, for instance, believed that the human mind contained 'unconscious' material, of which we are mostly unaware on a day-to-day basis, and they were interested to explain 'why' human beings are religious. However, they came to disagree with each other profoundly on certain issues, including the question of whether or not religion was 'a good thing', and they finally went their separate ways.

Explanations of why people might be religious can take different forms. Some explanations try to show why humans engage in such a meaningless activity which has no basis in reality. These sorts of explanations are known as reductive explanation or *reductionism*. Some psychological (and indeed, some sociological) explanations of religion are reductive. Another feature of reductive explanations is that the thing being explained (for us, religious behaviour) is explained in the terms of another discipline, and not in the terms of the thing in its own right. To put it another way, reductive psychological explanations of religion describe religion as a function or product of the human mind. Religious (non reductive) explanations describe religion as the result of revelation, religious experience, or enlightenment. Religious people might agree that the human mind plays an important role in religion, but they would be unlikely to accept that religion can be 'explained away' simply in terms of how the human mind works. Both Freud and Jung (to some extent) gave reductive explanations of religion, but in different ways. For Freud, religion was an illusion, the fact of which could be explained away by reference to his understanding of the human mind. For Jung the source of religion was to be found in the human unconscious, but this did not mean that religion was an illusion. Therefore Freud is much more clearly reductionistic than Jung. Freud's thought is given the label of **Psychoanalysis**, and Jung's is called **Analytical Psychology**.

Seminar topic

As you read the sections on Freud and Jung, discuss whether reductionistic explanations of religion are satisfactory.

Sigmund Freud 1856-1939

Carl Gustav Jung 1875-1961

Background

Sigmund Freud was born in 1856 and lived most of his life in Vienna, Austria. His family were Jewish. In 1938 he fled the Nazis to London, where he lived until he died the following year on 23rd September 1939. Biographers always look for how aspects of his life experience influenced the development of his theories.

Although his family were Jewish, Freud saw himself as a Jew by culture only. He was an athiest and did not believe in the tenets of the Jewish faith. However, he strongly identified with the Jewish community. Most of his friends were Jewish and he attended meetings of the B'nai Brith (Jewish Society). At university he studied medicine, which at that time was only just beginning to be strictly scientific in the sense of relying on the principle of cause and effect, and rejecting religious understandings of the nature of human physiology. He also worked in a research laboratory. In 1886 he opened a medical practice. His first book Studies on Hysteria, co-written with his colleague Josef Breuer, appeared in 1895, when he was 39 years old.

He had a peaceful family life with his wife and six children, despite being, by all accounts, a somewhat neurotic and obsessional character. He was an obsessive collector of sculpture; a compulsive smoker, despite it causing ill-health; and most of all, his biographers tell us, he was always convinced of his own rightness and very intolerant of anyone who would disagree with him. Interestingly, despite his antagonism towards religion, he was also superstitious, believing in numerology. He claimed to be ashamed of this, since it clearly went against his proposed theories.

Sculpture in Freud's study in London.

Freudian theory

Freud had numerous connected ideas about what the human mind was like and where certain kinds of behaviour come from. They are summed up in the diagram below. These are the concepts you will need to understand in order to grasp Freud's thinking.

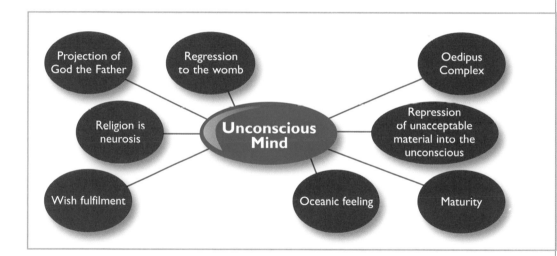

The Unconscious Mind

Religion as neurosis

In 1907 Freud wrote a paper entitled *Obsessive Acts and Religious Practices*, in which he describes religion as a **'universal obsessional neurosis.'**

> **Definition of neurosis:**
> a mental disorder, often associated with hysteria, anxiety, depression or obsessive behaviour

These ideas he later developed in his subsequent works, including *Totem and Taboo* (1913). There are numerous reasons why it seemed appropriate to Freud to describe religion in this way.

Religious activities bear a striking resemblance to the activities of a neurotic person. In neurotic conditions, often these day called OCD (Obsessive Compulsive Disorder), sufferers repeat actions which to the observer are meaningless; for example, excessive washing of hands, or other cleaning rituals, or a particular order of performing a complex task such as leaving the house (locking windows and doors and switching off lights) or going to bed. Michael Palmer states:

'Any deviation from these apparently trivial formalities will result in intolerable anxieties, dominated by a sense of guilt that they have not been performed. These ceremonies have indeed become 'sacred acts': no interruption of them will be tolerated and they are invariably performed in private.'
(Palmer, 1997, 13)

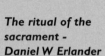

The ritual of the sacrament - Daniel W Erlander

For Freud the similarity between these kinds of behaviour, thought by society to be somehow unhealthy or deviant, and the behaviour of the religious person, was overwhelming. The reason why the neurotic is considered unhealthy is that their actions do not have a logical basis in fact. Constant, excessive, ritualistic hand-washing is not required to protect the human body from germs. The germs are an imagined focus for neurotic fear. Similarly in religion, rituals are repeated in relation to God who has no basis in fact. Just like the anxiety induced in the neurotic prevented from performing the neurotic activity, the religious person prevented from performing the required rituals is beset by guilt, a sense of their own 'sin', and fear of impending 'retribution.'

For Freud, psychological health, or what he termed 'maturity', would come about when people stopped indulging in this neurotic behaviour and faced life as it really is. The aim of life was to become adjusted to the scientific worldview and to leave all neurotic religious beliefs and practices behind.

Task

Writing tasks	a) In your own words, what are the similarities between neurotic behaviour and the performance of religious rituals? Try to think of at least 5 examples of possible neurotic behaviour, and possible religious rituals.
	b) How reasonable is Freud in drawing similarities between neurotic behaviour and religious ritual practice? Are there any problems with his theory? If you are struggling, turn to the section on 'Criticisms of Freud'.

Seminar topic

Is Freud right to claim that non-religious people are more 'mature' than religious people?

So if religious practices are merely neurotic behaviour, it seems reasonable to ask why then so many people perform them. What is wrong with the minds of the vast majority of humanity? After all, religion is found in every culture and throughout history. It is (as Freud himself acknowledged) virtually universal. To explain the fact of religious belief and practice, Freud had quite a complex theory of the human mind. First of all he understood it to contain unconscious material. He had very firm ideas (that have been widely criticised) about the nature of that material. He argued that the contents of the unconscious come out in strange distorted ways as 'projection'. The notion of God to be found in many religions is not actually real, but a projection from the unconscious mind. Humans, because they are weak and do not seek maturity, cling to this notion of God (whilst at the same time being afraid of it). In doing so they actually regress or go backwards in their development, away from personal maturity and autonomy, and towards, in Freud's terms, their mothers' wombs.

Let's look at some of these ideas in more detail.

The Unconscious Mind

Early in his career Freud and Josef Breuer worked with patients who had emotional disorders. In keeping with the new 'cause and effect' understanding of science, they argued that some traumatic event that the patient had forgotten had caused the emotional disorder. After the event, the person had *repressed* (this is an important piece of Freudian terminology) the memories. In other words these memories had gone into the unconscious mind, not available to the person on a daily basis, but still somehow 'there' and influencing their behaviour. Breuer's famous case of the hysterical woman, Anna O, whom he cured by enabling her to remember an event through hypnosis, was very influential in Freud's development of the theory of the Unconscious Mind.

Seminar topics

Consider other possible explanations of emotional and mental disorders which do not require the concept of the Unconscious Mind (e.g. chemical imbalance In the brain, genetic reasons, physical illness like Alzheimer's or Parkinson's, drug abuse).

How reasonable do you find Freud's understanding of the Unconscious Mind?

Note: If you are interested in some of Freud's cases you can read about them in *The Wolfman and Other Cases* (Penguin Classics, 2002)

For Freud every human being has an unconscious mind, and in order to attain 'maturity' or psychological health, the individual needs to face and come to terms with its contents. It makes sense to ask at this point 'what kind of material is to be found in the unconscious mind? In his work with numerous patients, such as in the case of Anna O, Freud discovered that the source of neurotic behaviour is in some kind of traumatic event, or some kind of childhood sexual experience or desire.

Human beings cannot face the idea that they have inappropriate sexual desires which are overwhelming in their power. Because of this, these feelings are repressed into the unconscious mind, and we are simply unaware of them. For Freud, however, it was not just isolated experiences which some humans might have had and others not; every human unconscious mind was made up of these latent but powerful desires, which Freud described as the Oedipus Complex. He even had a theory to explain why all humanity suffered from an Oedipus Complex.

The Oedipus Complex and the Primal Horde Theory

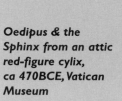

Oedipus & the Sphinx from an attic red-figure cylix, ca 470BCE, Vatican Museum

In the ancient Greek mythical story of Oedipus, to be found in Homer and other ancient writers, Oedipus is born to Laius and Jocasta. At his birth there was a prophecy which said that he would kill his father and marry his mother. To avoid this prophecy coming true, he was sent away to be killed, but the shepherd charged with his murder simply hung him up in a tree, and he survived. On a journey he met a man at a crossroads; they had a dispute and Oedipus killed the man, not knowing that he was his father, Laius.

When he arrived in Thebes, he solved the riddle set by the Sphinx who had previously tormented the city. In gratitude the Thebans made Oedipus their king, and gave him the hand of Jocasta as part of the reward, unbeknown to him or anyone that she was his mother. They had four children. Eventually though he discovered the truth from the shepherd, went mad and blinded himself. Jocasta killed herself.

Freud took this legend but used it in a different way, to claim that deep down in the unconscious mind, humans have a desire to kill their father and have sexual relations with their mother. He claimed that there was a historical reason for this. In his book Totem and Taboo he claimed that primitive humans had lived in groups or 'hordes' dominated by a powerful male who had sexual relations with all the women in the group and saw off any men who attempted to take what was his.

In Freud's theory, early in the history of humanity, the men of the horde, driven by desire, hatred and jealousy, got together and killed the father-figure, so that they could have access to the women. Then, overwhelmed with guilt for what they had done, they put a totem or symbol (in those days an animal) in the place of the father and made two rules: one, that no-one may kill the totem, and the other that no-one may commit incest (their original desire). For Freud this act was the beginning of religion. It explains the fact that in all humans (or at least in all men) there is an Oedipus complex that must be 'controlled', and that there is a symbolic figure which induces guilt and fear, but is also sacred and to be protected, i.e. God, who, by no coincidence, is thought to be 'Father' in the main monotheistic religions.

Projection

For Freud, God was nothing more than the projected contents of the unconscious mind: the sum of the repressed fear, guilt and desire of humanity stretching way back into history.

Projection is an interesting notion, and it could be argued that we do it all the time. Preconceived ideas in our own heads affect the way we see the world. Have you ever seen a celebrity in real life and thought they were taller and more radiant than those around them, or have you ever seen a spider running across a floor, only to find that in fact it was some fluff blowing in a draught? Our minds 'project' what we expect onto reality, often for quite emotional reasons. The celebrity is tall and radiant because of our desire, the fluff is a spider because of our innate fear. This desire and fear might be entirely unconscious but it affects how we see the world.

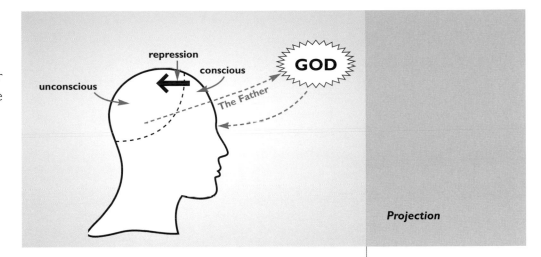

Projection

In Freud's thought, projection explained many emotional and psychological disturbances that could be cured by seeing their unconscious cause and talking about it (he called Psychoanalysis 'the talking cure'). It also explained what occurred in dreams. For Freud, figures and events in dreams were projections, and could give clues, if interpreted properly, to the contents of the unconscious mind. Most importantly for our study though, the figures and stories of religion, and in particular the figure of God, were projections from the unconscious mind, as a result of a repressed Oedipus Complex suffered by the whole of humanity since early in humanity's history. Of course, most people deny that these figures are projections from the unconscious mind. Freud called this 'negation', and argued it proved repression was still taking place.

Task

Writing task	How convincing is Freud's idea of 'projection'?

Seminar topic

As a group, can you think of any examples of projection which occur in your thinking about the world? This is a difficult question, because most of the time we are not aware that we are projecting!

For Freud not only religion, but also culture, was the product of material which was repressed into the unconscious mind. Much of human behaviour is 'sublimation'. For example the work of many artists comes from the sublimation of the contents of the unconscious. Sublimation means using the energy of sexual or destructive impulses in a way that is socially acceptable.

The Oceanic Feeling and wish-fulfilment

In a book called *Civilisation and its Discontents* Freud engages with a writer friend, Romain Rolland, who had told him about the mystical experience, to be found in many religious traditions, in which the mystic has the overwhelmingly powerful experience of him or herself becoming one with God or the Universe. Rolland had described this as the Oceanic Feeling, a term also used by the Hindu mystic Ramakrishna.

Ramakrishna, Hindu mystic and originator of the term 'the oceanic feeling'

Instead of finding this persuasive, Freud argues that in fact it is evidence of the true nature of religion which is mere 'wish-fulfilment.' This idea had also been a strong theme of his earlier book *The Future of an Illusion*. Humans cannot cope with life as independent beings. They find it isolating and threatening. As infants they did not need to be individuals with egos. They relied completely on their mother. The most comforting and connected state is, of course, inside the womb, where they are not even differentiated beings, let alone isolated. For Freud, the desire for the mystical experience, so celebrated in religions, is nothing more than the desire every human being has to return to the womb, to a sense of undifferentiated connectedness. It is characterised by the complete opposite of the quest for maturity: it is in fact regression. It is therefore highly ironic that this experience should be seen as the pinnacle of spiritual development.

Task

Writing task	Is Freud fair to accuse religion of being nothing more than wish-fulfilment?

Criticisms of Freud

Freud is in fact one of the most criticised of modern thinkers, and much research after his time has suggested that there are problems with the way he has understood religion.

Religion as universal neurosis

Research has shown that in fact religious people are less neurotic than others. Benjamin Beit-Hallahmi and Michael Argyle's book *The Psychology of Religious Behaviour, Belief and Experience (1997)* surveys much of this research. Religious people are in fact less likely than non-religious people to suffer with mental illness, to feel depressed or suicidal, or to be psychotic.

It is also possible to argue that if religion is universal, then it cannot be 'deviant' or something abnormal. It makes no sense to say 'most people are abnormal'. 'Most' people must define the norm.

Freud is also criticised for reducing religion to ritual. Whilst it might be argued that the excessive performance of rituals could be neurotic, religion is about so much more than ritual observance. In fact in most religions, the slavish performance of rituals in the belief that these will protect from damnation is strongly criticised.

The Oedipus Complex and Primal Horde Theory

Whilst some research has supported the idea of repression, Freud's Oedipus Complex theory it is still highly controversial. The idea of the Primal Horde has been totally repudiated. Freud's theory depends on the idea that characteristics are inherited from one generation to the next. This was the theory of the evolutionary scientist Jean-Baptiste Lamarck, whose work, even by Freud's time, was widely discredited. Freud obstinately held on to this view, not for scientific reasons, but because it helped to support the foundation of psychoanalysis. There was no evidence for the primal horde, the primal patricide, or for the genetic inheritance of guilt and fear. Although there was some evidence for totemism, it was by no means universal. It is particularly difficult to claim that a repressed Oedipus Complex is behind religion which is focused on a female deity, or in a matrilineal society (where females have authority). An Oedipus Complex could only account for a male God.

Freud is criticised for his very male-orientated view of society and of religion. He described women as suffering from penis envy, because they were effectively men without a penis. Part of the Oedipus Complex suffered by men involved fear that they would be castrated in retribution for their sin (i.e. the original sin of killing the father of the Primal Horde). This was the source of 'fear of God'. Freud thought that young boys would see women simply as castrated men, thus confirming the boys' fears. There has been (not surprisingly perhaps!) very little corroborating evidence for this theory.

Religion as wish-fulfilment

Freud saw religion as providing a kind of comfort-blanket. Many religious people would argue that whilst religion might at times be a great source of comfort, it is not the reason for being religious, and at times it is not true. Sometimes being religious makes people very vulnerable, say in situations of persecution or of bullying. Religion also requires facing up to ultimate questions about who we are and what happens when we die. It could be said that those with their heads in the sand just living lives of pleasure and materialism are really those seeking the comfort-blanket.

Religion as illusion

Of course the question of whether the claims of religion have any basis in fact has been argued down the centuries with no satisfactory conclusion. Freud may be right and religion may well be illusion. However, Freud is criticised for his simple assumption that illusion is bad and should be left behind. Many would argue that 'illusion', say in the form of art, imagination and creativity is actually positive. Religion might be a 'story', but perhaps it is a good story for a culture to have. To put it another way, the juxtaposition of reality and illusion in Freud is too marked. Those who take this view are often supporters of Jung's view of religion. (See Chapter 10.)

Orientation to a scientific worldview is progress

Freud claimed that when society moved away from religion and superstition and towards a scientific worldview, it would become healthy. History has seen some societies attempt to do this, such as the Communist Soviet Union and China. There is no evidence that these societies have been any healthier than ones which have retained religion. There is no evidence that a scientific outlook might be healthier than a religious one, and some evidence that the opposite is true.

Chapter 9

Seminar topic

What do you make of these objections to Freud's understanding of religion? Do they hold up?

Can anything in Freud's thought be salvaged from these criticisms?

Circular and reductionistic

Some people object to Freud's theory because his starting point is atheism, and his argument goes on to confirm that atheism. He is accused of a circular argument, which is biased from the very beginning. His theory is also 'reductionistic': it attempts to explain religion away (i.e. to explain why people indulge in this mistaken behaviour) in terms of a discipline which is completely outside of religion (i.e psychology). A non-reductionistic theory, which tried to look at religion in its own terms, would be preferable.

Some useful quotations from Freud's works

'If one wishes to form a true estimate of the full grandeur of religion, one must keep in mind what it undertakes to do for men. It gives them information about the source and origin of the universe, it assures them of protection and final happiness amid the changing vicissitudes of life, and it guides their thoughts and motions by means of precepts which are backed by the whole force of its authority.'
New Introductory Lectures on Psychoanalysis

'Religion is an illusion and it derives its strength from the fact that it falls in with our instinctual desires.'
New Introductory Lectures on Psychoanalysis

'Devout believers are safeguarded in a high degree against the risk of certain neurotic illnesses; their acceptance of the universal neurosis spares them the task of constructing a personal one.'
The Future of an Illusion

'At bottom God is nothing more than an exalted father.'
Totem and Taboo

'In the long run, nothing can withstand reason and experience, and the contradiction religion offers to both is palpable.'
The Future of an Illusion

'The more the fruits of knowledge become accessible to men the more widespread is the decline of religious belief.'
The Future of an Illusion

'It would be very nice if there were a God who created the world and was a benevolent providence, and if there were a moral order in the universe and an after-life; but it is a very striking fact that all this is exactly as we are bound to wish it to be.'
The Future of an Illusion

Glossary

analytical psychology	Jung's Psychological theory
illusion	Something which is believed in, but unlikely to be true. For Freud, religion was illusion
maturity	A state of psychological development in which the individual was adjusted to the scientific view of the universe and no longer projecting material from the unconscious mind
negation	The emergence of repressed material into the conscious mind, yet still denied by the individual
neurosis	Mental disorder associated with hysteria, anxiety, depression or obsessive repetitive behaviour
Oceanic feeling	The feeling reported by many mystics from the world's religious traditions of becoming one with God or with the universe. The term was used by Ramakrishna, and reported to Freud by Romain Rolland.
Oedipus Complex	Freud's theory which states that at an unconscious level men wish to have sexual relations with their mothers, and hate and fear (and want to kill) their fathers
Primal Horde Theory	To explain the existence of the Oedipus Complex, Freud argued that in earliest societies an act of patricide had occurred to enable sexual access to the females of the tribe (horde). In an expression of guilt for the murder, the father was replaced by a totem (symbol), and taboos were placed upon killing the totem and on incest. Moreover, the guilt from that original act remained a part of the make up of human beings from that time forward.
projection	The contents of the unconscious mind emerge, in distorted ways, often in dreams and religious beliefs, and also in relationships and daily life
psychoanalysis	Freud's psychological theory and method for achieving maturity
reductionism	Explaining a phenomenon in terms of a separate discourse, rather than describing it in its own terms
regression	The opposite of becoming mature. The desire to return to a womb-like state. Freud described the desire for religious experience as regression
repression	Pushing material that cannot be faced consciously into the unconscious mind
sublimation	Using the energy of sexual or destructive impulses in socially acceptable ways
taboo	A prohibition (for example on killing the totem or on incest)
totem	A symbol
wish fulfilment	The false belief that something is true just because we would like it to be

Jung

Aim

After studying this chapter you will have been introduced to Jung's understanding of religion, and will have engaged with it critically.

Background

Carl Gustav Jung was born in 1875 to a Swiss family. His father was a scholar and a pastor who had lost his faith but lacked the courage to leave his calling, and seemed to be a rather weak man. His mother was unhappy and may have suffered with mental illness. Carl, understandably perhaps, was a strange child, aloof and withdrawn, spending time in secret hideaways, living in his mind and having strange dreams.

Life improved for him when in 1895 he went to University in Basel and studied medicine, followed by psychiatry. Whilst there he made a study of his fifteen-year-old cousin Helen who claimed to be controlled by spirits, and when in a trance changed her accent completely, a phenomenon which fascinated Jung. This marked the beginning of an interest in the supernatural which was to remain with Jung for the rest of his life. Eventually Jung was to become a lecturer in Psychiatry at the University of Zurich, and in 1907 he met Sigmund Freud and became his disciple.

Initially for Jung, Freud was the father-figure he had really needed, after his own experience of the weakness and lack of character of his own father. However, for Freud, this was problematic, because to his mind sons have Oedipus Complexes and deep down wish to kill the father, and whilst he craved Jung's respect, he also felt very threatened by him. Over time, Jung found that he could not accept Freud's negative view of religion, and the way he reduced all human behaviour to sexuality. For Jung, Freud was not the sceptical scientist he claimed to be, but was, rather, dogmatic and irrational.

Jung's ideas began to develop along very different lines. Whilst Freud thought that religion was the mistaken projection of sexual material in the unconscious mind, Jung thought that religion was a reality at the psychic (unconscious) level. He also believed that religion was not a symptom of neurosis and immaturity, but actually necessary for individuation, the name given by Jung to the process of becoming psychologically whole and mature.

As Jung began to publish his ideas, a great rift developed between the two men, and in 1913 Jung resigned from his presidency of the Psychoanalytic Association founded by Freud,

Carl & Emma Jung

and they had no more contact. For the next four or five years, Jung suffered with some difficult psychological problems of his own, also, it is said, brought on by the problems in his marriage.

Jung had married Emma Rauschenbach in 1903, and they had four daughters and a son. Jung clearly loved Emma all his life, but he also loved a woman named Toni Wolff, whom he claimed to need for inspiration. He also surrounded himself with numerous other devoted women. Emma found this very difficult to accept, though she eventually did so. It was however, a traumatic time for them both. The psychological upheaval experienced by Jung in this period was also very creative, and most of his seminal ideas were born at this time.

Jungian Theory

Jung's theory owed a great deal to Freud's in that he accepted the notion of the unconscious mind, (though in a modified way) and believed that religion was projection from the unconscious. For Jung, though, this did not make religion an illusion as it did for Freud. Although the source of religion was the unconscious, this was a truer reality than that of external things. His understanding of the nature of the unconscious mind differed greatly too. His first great explanation of his theory came in his book *Symbols of Transformation* which was published in 1911.

The Collective Unconscious

For Freud, the unconscious mind contains the repressed material experienced by an individual that he or she is unable to face at the conscious level. For Jung, whilst there is a personal unconscious, the unconscious mind contains a great deal more material than that, and in fact most of the material is shared by all of humanity and is not repressed by individual experience. This vast area of the human psyche (mind) he termed the Collective Unconscious and said that it contained primordial images common to all humanity. These images he termed 'archetypes', and everybody has them. Children are not born with a blank psyche, but with these images in their unconscious minds.

These images, archetypes, or to put it another way, 'aspects of self', have a great deal of influence on how we relate to the world. The key to Jung's idea of psychological health was balance. If one archetype becomes dominant in the psyche, then the person suffers from neurosis, or even from schizophrenia. The journey to individuation required making the archetypes conscious; or, to put it another way, integrating the unconscious and the conscious mind.

The archetypes cannot be known directly, they are mysterious and inaccessible to conscious thought. However, they are projected outwards in the form of myths and symbols, and in this way they can be known. So for Jung, knowing and participating in religious symbols and narrative was absolutely crucial for understanding the archetypes. The archetypes are projected in other ways too. Dreams and daydreams (what Jung called visions) contain unconscious material, and if they are interpreted correctly they show the archetypes to the conscious mind. Also in our relationships with people in the world, we project, or as Jung put it, we 'actualise' archetypal material, usually without realising it.

The Archetypes

There are many archetypes, but some are particularly important:

The Persona

The Persona

The term persona refers to the mask a Classical Greek actor wore to identify their role. This is the archetype of the self that we present to the world, and relates to our role in life. We are 'a student', or 'a teacher'. If the persona archetype is too strong we have anxiety dreams about appearing naked in our place of work.

The Shadow

This archetype contains everything about us which we cannot face, and don't want to reveal. It contains our ability to perform actions which go against our moral principles, in other words the darker side of our persona. Because we can't face it as individuals, the shadow is often projected out as particular figures in cultures, such as the devil in religion, or 'baddies' in myths and stories, either ancient or modern. These figures seem particularly powerful to us because they tell us about our own potentiality for evil.

Jungian psychologists would describe the obsession some people have with brutal crimes not as a fascination with other people but as their journey to understand their own shadow. Once the reality of the shadow is faced at a conscious level, its power as an archetype is brought into balance with all the others, and it cannot rule us in secret from the depths of the unconscious mind.

When we are particularly repelled by a person, often for no apparent reason, Jung would say what is happening at the unconscious level is that we are projecting our own shadow onto that person, and are therefore horrified by it. It is a common way of thinking to say that we don't like people because they represent the characteristics we

The Shadow

don't like in ourselves. Jung would agree with this, and emphasise that we may be completely unaware of these characteristics or potentialities because they are at an unconscious level. When we don't like someone, we should be very interested in that experience because it is teaching us about our own unconscious drives.

The Anima and Animus

These are the female and male archetypes respectively. Both men and women have both. In general men have to make their anima conscious, and women, their animus. These archetypes can be known through relating to mythical or religious figures, or even symbols. The anima, for example, is represented in figures like Eve and the Virgin Mary in Christianity, or Shakti in Hinduism, but also in symbols such as the cave or ship. The animus is represented by the eagle, bull or tower; male characteristics of aggression and the phallus are obvious here.

The Animus

The anima and animus need to be in balance for psychological health, so the less dominant one of the two needs to be discovered. In Jungian thought, when men and women form partnerships, what is going on at the unconscious level is that the archetypes are reaching out for balance, through encounter with their opposite. Thus when a man is attracted to a woman, it is because she represents his anima characteristics with which he must become familiar. Jung described his attraction to Toni Wolff, his mistress, in terms of his need to relate to his own anima through her.

Task

Research and presentation task	Build a research portfolio of male and female symbols in religious narratives and myths. Give an explanatory presentation of your research findings.

The Wise Old Man

This archetype features in many myths and legends. Merlin in the stories of King Arthur, and Gandalf in *The Lord of the Rings* are wise old men. A modern version of the wise old man is Albus Dumbledore in the Harry Potter Stories.

The Wise Old Man

According to Jung, the reason such figures in myth and fiction have such power is because they are archetypal, in other words they are part of the structure of the psyche for all humanity. These figures are found in the myths and stories of every culture, enabling Jung to claim that the Collective Unconscious was Universal.

Other archetypes include the mother, the child, the father and so on. Also, certain events are archetypal, such as birth, marriage and death. When the representation of an archetype is encountered in the external world, the archetype in the unconscious mind

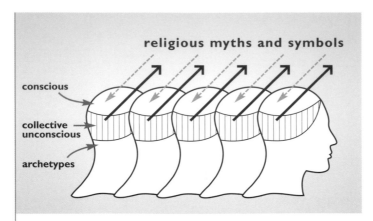

is activated, and can thereby become actualised, leading ultimately to individuation. The archetypes really form a blueprint of all human experience, and the task of life is, as far as is possible, to allow this blueprint to become reality.

The Self

For Jung, the Self (with a capital S) was the organising principle of the psyche (mind), so in a sense also archetypal. Antony Stevens says of the Self:

The Self

'*Its goal is wholeness, the complete realisation of the blueprint for human existence within the context of the life of the individual. Individuation is the raison d'etre of the self.*' (1994, 61)

This being the case, and religion being one of the best mechanisms by which individuation through the actualisation of the archetypes can take place, religion is of ultimate value to Jung. Unlike for Freud, for whom the presence of religion was neurosis, for Jung the absence of religion was a very bad sign for psychological health.

This notion of wholeness was for Jung best represented in the image of the mandala, which became for him the archetypal symbol of the self. Mandalas are found in one form or another in many religious and cultural traditions, and usually show some kind of organising principle around a central point. They are used ritually or in meditation to symbolise the journey to enlightenment, salvation or wholeness, also understood as a journey to the 'centre'. Only when all the outer components are taken account of can the journey to the centre occur. Dreams of circles or mandalas are very significant as they are glimpses of the very deep archetype of the Self.

Task

Research task	Find examples of mandalas. Do not restrict yourself only to the religions of Buddhism and Hinduism, where mandalas are easy to find, but explore other religious contexts too.

In Jung's thought, the figure of Christ was also a representation of the archetype of the Self. Because Christ is depicted in Christian art and narrative as a hero who overcomes great trials and is a perfect, whole, integrated man, (so perfect, in fact, that he is divine), he expresses the archetype of the self inherent in the Collective Unconscious of all humanity. It is reasonable to ask 'Did Jung believe in Christ?' One answer is that in a way, yes he did, as a symbolic psychic reality. For Jung psychic reality was the true reality. Christ is not a figure 'out there', either in history or in heaven, but 'in here' at the deepest, truest level. However, Jung also had an interesting understanding of the word 'believe', as we shall see in the next section.

Seminar topic

Consider ways in which Christians might react to Jung's understanding of Christ.

God as archetype of the Collective Unconscious

At a deeper level in the Collective Unconscious than even the Self, Jung argued that the God archetype was the core of all the symbols and imagery of God in the religions. As with the other archetypes, the God archetype cannot be known directly. It can only be known through symbols projected out from the Unconscious. Jung's claim is that this unknowable God archetype is a component of the Collective Unconscious, that is to say, everyone has it; it is universal.

A symbol for God found in many religions and cultures (such as Egyptian, Babylonian, Hindu, Platonic and Christian) is a triune, or three-fold deity. Because the trinity is symbolic of aspects of the self it is a potent symbol of the unknowable contents of the Collective Unconscious. For Jung, however, without the fourth element of the Shadow archetype (thus forming a 'quaternity') the human psyche cannot be considered 'whole'. Trinities in Jungian thought are but incomplete quaternities.

Symbols only work if they remain dynamic. If people think that symbols are merely representations of objective outer reality, they lose their power. Thus for Jung, much of organised religion had lost its meaning. The symbols had become what he called mere signs. They had lost their power to actualise the God archetype latent in the Collective Unconscious. This failure of organised religion was encapsulated for Jung in a dream he had as a boy, of God dumping a giant turd on Basel Cathedral. The meaning of this is obvious: that God despises organised, formalised, 'dead' religion.

Jung was asked whether he believed in God. His reply, both in interviews and in writing, was to say that if he were to express a 'belief' in something it would mean that he didn't 'know' it, and was simply expressing an opinion. He said:

> 'Either I know a thing and then I don't need to believe it because I am not sure that I know it. I am well satisfied with the fact that I know experiences which I cannot avoid calling numinous or divine.'
> Two Essays on Analytical Psychology: Collected Works 7, 215-16

To put it another way, Jung didn't believe in God, he knew him: but not as an external object, rather as a psychic truth.

Criticisms of Jung

Falsifiability

It is not possible to prove one way or the other whether the Collective Unconscious or the archetypes exist. Supporters of Jung claim plenty of evidence; detractors claim that this evidence can be interpreted differently. The Archive for Research in Archetypal

Symbolism has a huge database of mythological and ritualistic symbolism across cultures, drawing parallels which suggest that the human mind projects from a collective blueprint.

> **Note:** The Archive for Research in Archetypal Symbolism can be found at http://aras.org/

However, it is equally possible to explain these similarities in different ways (for example, contact between cultures leading to the transmission and sharing of ideas.) Very often the way Jung writes about the Unconscious and the Archetypes is very obscure and mystical, leading to the impression that he is unscientific in his methods.

Individuation

For Jung, the goal and purpose of life was Individuation; the integrating of the contents of the Unconscious Mind with the Conscious Mind, knowing all the archetypes, and having them in balance. It is debatable whether this goal is the same as the goal of religion. Jung's goal seems psychotherapeutic. The goals of religion are metaphysical, and to do with salvation or liberation. Jungians may consider these goals to be the same thing. Many religious people would not.

The Psychic Reality of God

In all of his work, Jung is very careful not to claim the objective, metaphysical reality of God. God is certainly 'real' but an internal, shared, psychic reality. This is seen by some of his critics as merely a subjective claim, based on a circular argument. To claim God is real, but not 'out there' is not meaningful for some people.

Task

Writing task	Do you agree with Jung's positive assessment of religion? Give reasons for your answer.

Seminar topic

Prepare for and stage a debate on the following topic:

'Jung's understanding of religion is better than Freud's.'

Both teams should marshal and present their arguments either for or against the statement, and the statement should be put to the class for a vote.

Some useful quotations from Jung's works

'It is the face of our own shadow that glowers at us across the Iron Curtain.'
Man and His Symbols

'A more or less superficial layer of the unconscious is undoubtedly personal. I call it the "personal unconscious". But this personal layer rests upon a deeper layer, which does not derive from personal experience and is not a personal acquisition but is inborn. This deeper layer I call the "collective unconscious". I have chosen the term "collective" because this part of the unconscious is not individual but universal; in contrast to the personal psyche, it has contents and modes of behaviour that are more or less the same everywhere and in all individuals.'
The Archetypes and the Collective Unconscious

'Because we cannot discover God's throne in the sky with a radiotelescope or establish (for certain) that a beloved father or mother is still about in a more or less corporeal form, people assume that such ideas are "not true." I would rather say that they are not "true" enough, for these are conceptions of a kind that have accompanied human life

from prehistoric times, and that still break through into consciousness at any provocation.'
Man and His Symbols

'The meeting of two personalities is like the contact of two chemical substances: if there is any reaction, both are transformed.'
Modern Man in Search of a Soul

'The unconscious is not just evil by nature, it is also the source of the highest good: not only dark but also light, not only bestial, semihuman, and demonic but superhuman, spiritual, and, in the classical sense of the word, "divine."'
The Practice of Psychotherapy

'The dream is the small hidden door in the deepest and most intimate sanctum of the soul.'
The Meaning of Psychology for Modern Man

'I could not say I believe— I know! I have had the experience of being gripped by something that is stronger than myself, something that people call God.'
Face to Face interview with John Freeman in 1959

'Knowing your own darkness is the best method for dealing with the darknesses of other people.'
Source Unknown

'People will do anything, no matter how absurd, in order to avoid facing their own soul.'
Source Unknown

Some reflections on the Psychology of Religion

Freud's Psychoanalysis and Jung's Analytical Psychology are but two amongst many forms of psychology with perspectives to offer on questions about religions. Often Freud and, to a lesser extent, Jung are criticised because their interest in religious behaviour came at first from an interest in psychologically sick people. These days psychologists of religion are interested in the full spectrum of people, both sick and healthy, and indeed are sometimes critical of the terms 'sick' and 'healthy'.

Many psychologists are interested in the various links between personality and religion. They ask what kind of people are religious? What other characteristics do they show? Do some personality types become attracted to certain types of religion, and others to other types? What happens to people when they lose their faith? Some psychologists are interested in the actual events which occur in the brain at the moment of a religious experience. What links them all however is the focus on the individual and on the human mind.

If we are to study religion it is important to ask whether a psychological approach to religion is enough. We have seen from our study of Freud and Jung, that Freud dismissed God's existence, and Jung accepted a form very different to that described in many religions. Have they solved the question of whether or not God exists? Or is that question still open to discussion by philosophers, natural scientists, theologians, poets, artists, humans in general?

What other disciplines are important to the study of religion? Clearly a useful companion to psychology is sociology. Whereas psychology looks for the relationship between religion and the individual, sociology looks for the links between religion and society, and society's norms and institutions. Both disciplines use theories and models to describe religious behaviour, and some of these theories are 'functionalist' (explain religion in terms of its function) or 'reductionist' (explain it away).

Philosophy, however, tackles the truth claims of religion head-on and asks whether they make sense, or whether they could be 'true'. Phenomenology, on the other hand, tries to understand religious belief and behaviour, regardless of whether it is true or not. Of course there are many other disciplines and approaches in the study of religion. Perhaps a multidisciplinary approach has much to recommend it.

Task

Writing task	What can the psychology of religion offer to our understanding of religion? What are its limitations?

Glossary

anima	The female archetype
animus	The male archetype
archetypes	Aspects of self, which are expressed through myths and symbols, and in dreams and daily life
Collective Unconscious	The unconscious mind that is shared by all humanity
dream/vision	The means by which the collective unconscious may be known (visions are daydreams)
individuation	The process of integrating the unconscious mind into the conscious mind, and bringing the archetypes into balance
myth	Stories with archetypal components
Persona	The archetype of the self shown to the world
psychological balance	The aim of life, along with individuation. If the archetypes are balanced then there is psychological health
Self	The organising principle of the mind. One of the archetypes
Shadow	The archetype which expresses the evil of which each person is capable
symbol	The expression of an archetype; how it might appear in a dream, or in art, or in religious art or narrative

Bibliography

Section 1

Chapter 1

Bowie, Robert, *Ethical Studies (Second Edition),* Nelson Thornes, 2004, (978-0748780792)

Goddard, Andrew, *A Pocket Guide to Ethical Issues,* Lion Hudson Plc, 2006, (978-0745951584)

Luhman, Reg, *Euthanasia,* Abacus Educational Services, 1999, (978-1898653165)

Morgan, Peggy and Lawton, Clive A., *Ethical Issues in Six Religious Traditions (Second Edition),* Edinburgh University Press, 2007 (978-0748623303)

Thompson, Mel, *Teach Yourself Ethics,* Teach Yourself Books, 2006, (978-0349926963)

Vardy, Peter and Grosch, Paul, *The Puzzle of Ethics,* Fount Paperbacks, 1999, (978-0006281443)

Williams, Bernard (Editor), *One World Many Issues (New Edition),* Nelson Thornes, 2001, (978-0748762576)

Chapter 2

Bowie, Robert, *Ethical Studies (Second Edition),* Nelson Thornes, 2004, (978-0748780792)

Cole, W. Owen (Editor), *Moral Issues in Six Religions (Examining Religions),* Heinemann Educational Publishers, 1991, (978-0435302993)

Goddard, Andrew, *A Pocket Guide to Ethical Issues,* Lion Hudson Plc, 2006, (978-0745951584)

Jenkins, Joe, *Heinemann Advanced Religious Studies: Ethics & Religion (Second Edition),* Heinemann Educational Publishers, 2003, (978-0435303679)

Thompson, Mel, *Teach Yourself Ethics,* Teach Yourself Books, 2006, (978-0349926963)

Vardy, Peter and Grosch, Paul, *The Puzzle of Ethics,* Fount Paperbacks, 1999, (978-0006281443)

Walker, Joe, *Environmental Ethics,* Hodder Murray, 2000 (978-0340757703)

Section 2

Pinsky, Mark I. (2007), *The Gospel According to the Simpsons: Bigger And Possibly Even Better!* Edition (Westminster John Knox Press) 978-0-664-23265-8

Websites

www.bbc.co.uk/religion the bbc's homepage for all matters relating to religion

www.ofcom.org.uk the television regulator's homepage

www.hollywoodjesus.com useful, multi-faith sensitive, popular culture review site

www.fox.co.uk/thesimpsons   Official site of show, with many useful references

http://www.snpp.com   The Simpsons Archive - everything you could ever need for a study of The Simpsons.

Recommended viewing

Other soap operas may be used, but these are probably the best known:

- EastEnders (BBC1)
- Coronation Street (ITV1)
- Emmerdale (ITV1)
- Hollyoaks (Channel 4/S4C)
- Pobol y Cwm (S4C)

Section 3

Davie, Grace, *The Sociology of Religion (New Horizons in Sociology)*, SAGE Publications, 2007 (978-0761948926)

Haralambos, Michael, Heald, R.M., and Holborn, Martin, *Sociology Themes and Perspectives (section on Religion)*, Collins Educational, 2004 (978-0007154470)

Moore, Stephen, Aiken, Dave and Chapman, Steve, *Sociology for A2 (unit on Religion)*, Collins Educational, 2002 (978-0007134656)

Partridge, Christopher (ed), *Encyclopedia of New Religions*, Lion Hudson, 2006 (978- 0745952192)

Selfe, P.L. and Starbuck, Mark, *Religion (Access to Sociology)*, Hodder Arnold, 1998 (978-0340711828)

Section 4

Appignanesi, Richard and Zarate, Oscar, (2007) *Introducing Freud*, Cambridge, Icon Books

Connolly, Peter, 1999 *'Psychological Approaches' in Connolly P.* (ed) Approaches to the Study of Religion, London, Cassell

Palmer, Michael, (1997) *Freud and Jung on Religion*, London, Routledge

Hyde, Maggie and McGuiness, Michael (2004) *Introducing Jung Cambridge*, Icon Books

Stevens, Antony, (1994) *Jung: A Very Short Introduction*, Oxford, Oxford University Press

Storr, Anthony (1989) *Freud: A Very Short Introduction*, Oxford, Oxford University Press

Useful websites

The Freud Museum in London   **http://www.freud.org.uk/**

The Archive for Research in Archetypal Symbolism   **http://aras.org/**

Films

Matter of Heart (1986) – the Life of Jung

Freud (2005) starring Michael Kitchen

Face to Face (1959) – interview with Jung by John Freeman